LEARNING
TO HELP

LEARNING TO HELP

BASIC SKILLS EXERCISES

PHILIP PRIESTLEY
JAMES McGUIRE

TAVISTOCK PUBLICATIONS
LONDON AND NEW YORK

First published in 1983 by
Tavistock Publications Ltd
11 New Fetter Lane, London EC4P 4EE
Published in the USA by
Tavistock Publications
in association with Methuen, Inc.
733 Third Avenue, New York, NY 10017

© *1983 Philip Priestley and James McGuire*

Typeset by
Scarborough Typesetting Services
and printed in Great Britain at the
University Press, Cambridge

British Library Cataloguing in Publication Data

Priestley, Philip
Learning to help.
1. Counselling
I. Title.   II. McGuire, James
361.3'23   BF636.C6

ISBN 0–422–77470–7
ISBN 0–422–77480–4 Pbk

Library of Congress Cataloging in Publication Data
Priestley, Philip.
Learning to help.
Includes bibliographical references and indexes.
1. Helping behavior.   2. Helping behavior—
Problems, exercises, etc.
I. McGuire, James.   II. Title.
BF637.H4P74   1983   158'.3   82–18860

ISBN 0–422–77470–7
ISBN 0–422–77480–4 (pbk.)

Acknowledgements

Our interest in teaching helping skills was first aroused by some work we did in 1975, when we were invited to train prison officers to work on a project to prepare men for leaving prison. The project led to the formulation of the ideas presented in a previous Tavistock publication, *Social Skills and Personal Problem Solving* (1978). For the origins of the material in this book, therefore, we are indebted to the stimulus of that work and all our colleagues in it, from the Industrial Training Research Unit in Cambridge, from Ranby and Ashwell prisons, and from the Day Training Centre in Sheffield.

For help in trying out some of the exercises we are grateful to members of a Bristol University Extra-Mural class in the autumn of 1980, and to all those people who joined us at the Langfords Hotel, Brighton. Chris Morgan, Celia Smith, and Fiona Bartels-Ellis made useful suggestions; Fred Bascombe and Frances Fox gave useful advice; and Rose Millington supplied ideas. Judy Oldham typed a lot of the text. Photographs were taken by Gordon Kelsey and David Roberts of the Photography Unit, University of Bristol, and the following people appear in them: Sarah Clark, Caroline Close, Julia Collins, Pam Haines, Janice Jobling, Steve Jolly, Anthony Knivett, Bronwen Owens, Helen Royall, Evan Scott-Batey, Peter Wright, and Peter Wilson. Thanks to them all.

PHILIP PRIESTLEY
JAMES McGUIRE

Contents

The true object of education, like that of every other moral process, is the generation of human happiness.

WILLIAM GODWIN, *The Enquirer*

A note on nomenclature

One of the problems in writing a book such as this is the lack of any really appropriate word for referring to the people on the receiving end of professional helping endeavours. We need a word which has universal applicability but which is also reasonably dignified as a means of denoting human beings with problems of some kind. Existing terms are almost all unsatisfactory for different reasons. 'Cases' still smacks of psychiatric stigma and still conjures up images of bizarre symptoms or highly infectious diseases. 'Client', the common currency in most social work agencies, based as it is on psychoanalytic concepts of helping, rings of therapy, or perhaps of legal representations, and certainly of the payment of fees. 'Helpee' sounds artificial and contrived, while other words such as 'patient', 'trainee', 'probationer', or the like have restricted definitions associated with particular occupations.

Finally, there are a number of more or less neutral words and phrases, such as 'individual', 'participant', 'group member', 'person with the problem', which although not, perhaps, very vivid in their portrayals of those receiving help, nevertheless have the advantage that they do not imply anything about a helping relationship other than the fact that it is what it is – an encounter in which one human being (who is most likely paid to do so) tries to give assistance to another. In this book we have tried, therefore, to use words of this kind, varying them as much as possible to avoid boredom and repetitiveness and to suit the contexts in which they occur.

1 Learning to help: a learning model

There is a school of thought which holds that helpers are born and not made. It is a view that places great emphasis on the personal qualities of whoever assumes the helping role; who should be warm, wise, understanding, sympathetic, articulate, intelligent. . . . Anyone who possessed all, or even a few of these attributes would naturally be a better helper than someone with none of them, but carried to extremes this point of view becomes an argument against the ability of more ordinary mortals to help each other, which is clearly untenable. Most of the helping that goes on in the world is between unaided individuals, in families, amongst friends, in neighbourhoods, and at work. Although it is unorganized and officially unacknowledged, it is a lubricant that makes the daily round not only possible but also a little more tolerable.

Impromptu acts of mutual aid and assistance to family members and friends are, however, different in kind from the work carried out in helping agencies, whether on a paid or an unpaid basis. The most important difference is that, to begin with at least, the people who turn to social agencies for help are perfect strangers to the people who work there. No ties of affection or shared experience exist between them, and any 'help' is given on a disinterested basis. The employed helper also spends the greater part of the working day engaged in activities (such as listening to other people's troubles and offering words of comfort or advice) which might occupy only a small proportion of the ordinary person's time. And those who approach helping agencies do so with an expectation, whether well founded or not, that they will receive a minimum level of service. If they are fortunate they will do even better than that, but with friends or relatives they can entertain no legitimate expectations about the quality of the help they will receive. It is this difference in 'quality' which is the starting point of this book, and it is principally concerned with what helpers *do* and how well they do it, rather than with the kinds of people they happen to *be* or hope to become. It concentrates on actual *helping behaviour* and on ways of developing and improving its effectiveness. The exercises in it are designed for use by would-be helpers of all kinds, whether they are on formal training courses or not; by tutors, trainers, and teachers on such courses; and by helpers working in the field who wish to examine and improve one or more aspects of their helping behaviour.

The idea of training helpers is not, of course, a new one. Social work education has adopted a 'professional' training model that combines 'theory' (typically, lectures on social work method, social policy, law, psychology, sociology, human growth and development) with 'practice' (usually supervised placements working with small numbers of cases in helping agencies) (Yelloly 1980). Trainers with interests in psychoanalysis have attempted to use both 'theory' and 'practice' as opportunities to develop the personality of the trainee helper by processes resembling those of a 'training analysis' (Towle 1954). More often, though, there has been a gap between the two which this book seeks to bridge by borrowing techniques from two other traditions of training: those devoted to industrial skills on the one hand, and to social skills on the other.

Industrial training employs a number of methods for producing skilled or competent workers. The longest lasting and most widespread of these has been the craft-apprentice model, a highly personal and extended learning process suited to a broad spectrum of complex skills as deployed in small-scale or batch production. Large-scale, mechanized industry, by contrast, demands a different training style and since the necessary skills are generally of a lower order, they can be taught by direct instruction and demonstration. When this was performed by skilled fellow workers it attracted the description of 'sitting by Nellie' from trainers who thought it 'unscientific' and who substituted for it what they have termed a 'micro-skills' approach (Seymour 1966). This starts with a minute analysis of the required occupational behaviour broken down into its smallest constituent parts. These are learned separately and then progressively reassembled into a skilled execution of more complex skills. Most programmes of skill training in this tradition combine direct instruction about what to do – with or without some background information (or 'theory'); watching and copying a skilled performer; and practice exercises of varying length and difficulty.

These and similar procedures can be located within a simple framework for training:

1 Definition of the behaviour to be taught and learned.
2 Analysis of the behaviour into some of its smaller component parts.
3 Instruction, and demonstration, of the relevant operations.
4 Practice by the learner until an acceptable standard of performance is reached.

Although this framework was developed for training in physical and mechanical skills, it can quite easily be adapted for use in less tangible areas of occupational behaviour such as dealing with the public, selling, interviewing, negotiating, making decisions, and management (Rackham and Morgan 1977). In non-commercial environments a similar approach can be used to train nurses, doctors, teachers, and prison officers to interact more effectively with other people (Ellis 1980).

Work in these areas has contributed to, and in turn drawn from, a parallel and more recent tradition of social skills training. This began with attempts to teach the basics of interaction to long-term psychiatric patients who had fallen out of practice in the everyday arts of conversation, and to help socially phobic individuals overcome some of their difficulties (Falloon, Lindley, and McDonald 1974). Behind these clinical developments lay social learning theory; a set of ideas opposed to the notion that social behaviour is *either* the outward expression of inborn and immutable traits of character *or* the product of blind processes of reward and punishment. Social learning theory asserts that everyday interaction relies on a repertoire of learned behaviours, some of them acquired unthinkingly, others being adopted, shaped, and retained according to the conscious wishes, preferences, and choices of the individuals concerned (Rotter 1954). So although a lot of behaviour is absorbed without conscious effort, rather like a child learning its mother tongue, it is still possible for the underlying mechanisms by which this is achieved to be made explicit and brought under the control of the learner, as in elocution lessons or learning a foreign language.

This process can be illustrated by the discoveries which were made when actual behaviour in social encounters was subjected to the same kind of close scrutiny as industrial skills. Some previously unrecognized dimensions of social behaviour were disclosed which have come to be called 'non-verbal communication' or nvc (Argyle 1975). It is not difficult to exaggerate, as some observers do (Morris 1977), the extent or significance of 'body language' but it is undeniable that posture, gesture, gaze, facial expression, and voice tone contribute significantly to the messages that are exchanged during social interaction. It is also the case that when some of these features of peoples' performances are brought to their attention, they are able to eliminate or change what they think undesirable in them.

So the first steps in social skills training consist of breaking down interaction into some of its simpler component parts and making some assessment of how particular individuals perform them. This can be done by a trainer who watches the behaviour, or by the person concerned watching a video tape-recording. The deficits or imperfections thus revealed become the focus of the training that follows, which resembles closely the industrial pattern of *instruction, demonstration,* and *practice* (Trower, Bryant, and Argyle 1978).

The trainer may give *instruction* by pointing out some of the basic rules of social interaction and the ways in which the learner may be failing to observe some of them, together with suggestions about how to do so more effectively. *Demonstration* can also be provided by a trainer but is more often and more usefully performed by someone who is selected to resemble the learner in as many characteristics as possible, except that of the desired behaviour, at which he or she should be more skilled. This kind of demonstrator is known as a 'model' and the process of demonstration as 'modelling' (Bandura 1962). In some cases, exposure to models may be all that is required, but it is more usual for a period of *practice* or rehearsal to prove necessary. This may initially take the form of role-play with peers or trainers and move only gradually towards practice in the real world. But rehearsal or practice by itself may become merely unreflective repetition, and the key to improved performance is *'feedback'*, information received from the social environment about the quality of someone's behaviour (Wiener 1950). In ordinary interaction much of this information is conveyed indirectly by nods and winks and other subtle cues which a socially inept person may fail to perceive. In social skills training these signals must be given directly to the learner, either by observers, or by the self-rating or self-monitoring of behaviour.

The self-consciousness evoked by all these procedures of scrutiny and critical appraisal is, however, only intended to be temporary. If the training is successful and performances improve and observed results get better, then the self-conscious nature of the behaviour is gradually transformed into a higher and almost automatic level of skill.

The exercises in this book are based on this model of learning and skill development. They begin by inviting readers to make their own definitions of helping behaviour and their motives for doing it. In the three major chapters that follow there are exercises for breaking down the complex skills of *interviewing, counselling,* and *group leading,* into some of their simpler component parts, together with methods for assessing levels of existing competence in each of them. Other materials propose ways of developing and improving these skills, using continuous feedback to monitor whatever progress is being made. The actual mechanics of improvement – the hard work of practice – must be supplied by the learner. We can offer no instant tips or magical insights which will transform the novice into a skilled helper overnight.

Nor does the book present anything that resembles a recommended model of 'good practice'. The best examples of good helping are to be found in the varied and idiosyncratic working styles of all manner of individuals (Hugman 1977). Those who are learning to help must first of all construct their own definitions of what they want to do. They must also establish the criteria by which to judge the quality of their performance and gather information from as many sources as possible about the effectiveness of what they are doing. They should also treat the materials and methods in the book in the same spirit; that is as starting points for their own training programmes, and not as a fixed and final curriculum for the production of 'identikit' helpers. So feel free to accept or reject particular exercises; to pick and choose those that promise the best opportunities for learning; to change and adapt the content to different topics or settings; to use them, in other words, in ways best suited to your own learning needs.

2 Defining the job: activities and values

Behaviour of any kind never exists in a vacuum; it is always affected and influenced by mental events of various kinds; the values and attitudes held by the actors; their feelings and emotions. The purpose of the exercises in this chapter is to help helpers look at how their own beliefs impinge on the work they do with people. Like many human activities, helping does not lend itself to neat or simple definition. The Oxford Dictionary makes several attempts:

— 'To furnish (a person, etc.) with what is serviceable to his efforts or needs; to aid or assist.'
— 'To add one's own action or effort to that of (another) so as to make it more effectual; to further the action or purpose of.'
— 'To supply or relieve the wants or necessities of; to succour.'
— 'To afford aid or assistance.'
— 'To benefit, do good to, to be of use or service to, to profit.'
— 'To succour in some distress or misfortune; hence to deliver, save, set free, relieve.'

Two main ideas are embedded in these definitions; first, the relief of distress by direct giving – the more intense the distress the more active the role of the helper – and second, the notion of working alongside people, aiding and seconding their efforts to help themselves. One dimension along which helping efforts can be arranged, therefore, stretches from helpless receipt at one end to sturdy self-help at the other. Another is defined by the extent to which the help succeeds in liberating its recipients from the conditions which made it necessary in the first place.

A more concrete description of what some sorts of employed helpers do is given in the

Classification of Occupations and Directory of Occupational Titles (CODOT) published by Her Majesty's Stationery Office:

> '*Social case-worker (general)*
> Helps individuals and/or families to overcome or lessen problems which arise in more than one field of social work within the scope of the social services.
>
> Ascertains nature, extent and root cause of problem by interviews and by any other available means; considers all factors involved, for example, relationships, environment, health and finance and decides on most satisfactory form of assistance; gives or arranges for such assistance which may include material or financial help; specialised advice and reference to appropriate social welfare bodies; encourages and promotes any necessary adjustment of social and personal attitudes; follows progress of cases after immediate problems have been solved; keeps case records and prepares requisite reports.'

This very full list may include duties which do not apply to all helpers; school and careers counsellors, for example, or workers in advice and information services; and they will apply in different degrees to other workers depending on the agencies they work for, the precise nature of their roles within them, their own interpretation of what they are supposed to do, and numerous other factors besides.

A helping diary

The first step in deciding what it is that helpers do, and might like to do better, is to keep a diary which records the activities of a representative period of time – a day, a week, a month, for example. An attempt should be made, when compiling a diary like this, to record the duration of each type of activity each day so that at the end of the week or the month it is possible to arrive at a total amount of time which has been devoted to it. The results can then be examined in a critical way. The most obvious thing to look for is the proportion of a helper's time that is taken up with 'face-to-face' work compared with that given over to more administrative chores such as writing, telephoning, or attending meetings. Not that these other activities are not necessary, but it can be instructive to look at the ratio of time spent in the two forms of behaviour.

Find out out what helpers do

If you are not presently employed as a helper this exercise can be completed by securing the co-operation of someone who is, and is willing to fill in a diary and share the results with an outsider. If you hope to work in a particular helping agency, it would make sense to approach someone already in post there, to *either* fill in a diary *or* to answer some questions.

Day	Social Services Office
Thursday, 4th February	**9.00 a.m.** Arrive at office. Phone call to foster-parent to arrange visit for next week. **9.05 a.m.** Collect current paper-work and also today's post and any messages. Sort out priorities and decide on any necessary action. **9.30 a.m.** Above task unfinished but time for team meeting - a regular weekly meeting of all social workers in team with senior social worker. Discussion this week included covering the work of colleague who will be absent for four weeks on a study fellowship. Also discussion about pending foster-parent applications and their allocation. **10.30 a.m.** Team meeting completed, cup of coffee made and continue with paper-work. Tried to make two phone calls but with no success. Read quickly details of case in preparation for 12 o'clock appointment. **11.00 a.m.** Office meeting for all social work staff. Routine fortnightly business meeting - topics included staffing matters, discussion of minutes of senior management meeting. **11.45 a.m.** I left to go to local police station. **12.00 noon** Appointment with local superintendent to discuss police decision to prosecute juvenile. I am doing social enquiry report and believe the matter could be dealt with by way of caution. **12.15 p.m.** Left police station, dictated note of meeting and drove home for lunch. **1.30 p.m.** Arrived back at office, dictated record of previous day's visits — yesterday was a particularly heavy day on visits. **3.00 p.m.** Recording not completed but out on visits again. **3.15 p.m.** Arrived for first visit. No appointment. No answer. On to the next. **3.25 p.m.** Visited 16-year-old lad who is subject to care order and who hadn't been to work for the last three days. **4.20 pm.** Visit completed. **4.30 p.m.** Arrived for next visit to foster placement to see 16-year-old lad. **5.45 p.m.** Visit finished. Drive home. As always at the end of the day lots of loose ends.

If you are able to interview a helper, or to reflect on your own experience, answers to some of the following questions would be useful.

— What do helpers actually do?
— What is the purpose of each activity?
— What are their outcomes: for the recipient?
                           for the helper?
                           for the agency?

The information gleaned from such an interview, or from keeping and studying a personal diary, can then be used to construct a job description.

Job description

A job description is simply a list of the tasks which are performed by the job holder. Quite often the ones provided by employers as a guide to prospective employees are more the products of wishful thinking on their part than of concrete data collection from the people who actually do the work.

A job description for a school careers counsellor might look like this:

— Interviews all fifth-year leavers at the beginning of the autumn term.
— Administers written aptitude tests and occupational interest blanks for each leaver; scores, analyses, and interprets the results to individuals concerned. Suggests possible occupations.
— Provides information on a personal basis concerning career choices.
— Maintains and extends school careers library and information services.
— Organizes careers talks, conventions, and visits.
— Arranges interviews with employers and training centres.
— Helps to resolve difficult career choices by providing information and by personal counselling.
— Runs leavers' groups to discuss problems.
— Provides training in interview techniques.
— Keeps records on all leavers.

A description for a residential social worker might look like this:

— Gets children up in morning in time for school.
— Supervises breakfast and other meals.
— Copes with sick children.
— Co-operates with schools over education of children.
— Deals with crises; bullying, tempers, moods, shouting, crying, screaming, tantrums, stealing, bed-wetting, running away, etc.
— Communicates with parents.

— Talks to field social workers.
— Attends staff meetings to discuss home policy and individual children.

Every item on a list like this could be broken down further into smaller component parts for the purpose of devising training exercises for newcomers to these fields.

☐ Write out a job description like these for the helping work that you do or hope to do. Discuss the items in it with someone else who does that job. Make some initial estimate of how well you perform each of the tasks in the description.

Values and attitudes

Although this book is about helping *behaviour*, it also acknowledges the vital role that ideas play in virtually everything we do. The beliefs we hold and the attitudes we take to the personal and social worlds we inhabit are powerful influences on conduct. These influences are not, however, always easy to trace since attitudes and values, like behaviour, are assumed and absorbed by processes of which we are not necessarily aware at the time. They are an omnipresent part of the atmosphere in families, at school and work, in friendship and leisure groups, and in the constant murmurings of the various media. The content of these messages is also extremely varied and the ways in which they are selected and then incorporated into the mental structures of individuals are barely understood.

The aim of the exercises in this section is to encourage helpers to look closely at their own attitudes and values and to decide to what extent they are relevant to the work they do and how far they contribute to its effectiveness or otherwise. The spirit in which this is proposed is not one that looks on motives for helping as somehow suspect or as projections of concealed need or deviant identification – there *are* individuals who choose to help others for odd reasons, but they are unlikely to amount to more than a tiny minority. It is simply that unacknowledged values and attitudes may create problems in dealing with certain kinds of people and may point helping efforts in directions not justified by the facts of a case. And because, in this country, a great deal of helping takes place within a framework of statutory and coercive powers, it can happen that the theories and ideas of agency employees are foisted on the recipients of their services without their knowledge or consent. A keener appreciation of one's own views is a pre-condition of effective helping and of communication free from gross misunderstanding, but it does not mean committing oneself to any ready-made ideology or narrow theory of helping.

☐☐ Defining values
These exercises are intended to elicit statements about some of your values in your own words and to make some suggestions about ways of sorting out and making sense of what you have said.

☐ **Complete the sentence:**

PEOPLE NEED HELP IN ORDER TO ....

Repeat the procedure *ten* times, completing the sentence differently each time, and writing down the responses on a sheet of paper.

☐ Working in pairs, interview each other and obtain at least five statements from your partner that answer the question:

I WOULD LIKE TO HELP PEOPLE BECAUSE..

Write a brief report of these statements in summary of the interview; adding what you think they tell you about your partner's motivation to help.

☐ Take a tape-recorder and a watch with you to a private place. Switch on the recorder and talk into it for one minute starting with the phrase:

WHAT'S WRONG WITH THE WORLD TODAY IS THAT ....

If you don't have a tape-recorder − or a friend − all three exercises can be done as written sentence completions. Whichever way you do it, the end product will be a quantity of evidence about your views on helping and your reasons for wanting to do it. This can be reviewed in a number of ways; simply reading or listening to it and thinking about it in a reflective way can be useful. Alternatively, or in addition, some attempt can be made to assign the statements you have made to a number of categories.

One of the most basic dimensions along which views of the outside world often seem to fall is one that can be characterized as *self-control* v. *external control*. Someone at the self-controlling end of the spectrum might take the view: 'Any success we enjoy in life is largely due to our own hard work.' A more fatalistic person might say something like: 'It's not *what* you know, but *who* you know that counts in life.' The first statement stresses the ability of the individual to shape his or her own destiny; the second tends to deny it. A number of instruments have been devised to measure this attitude towards the world, many of them requiring the services of an authorized psychological tester. A less precise, but still useful, way of determining your own position along this continuum is to answer the following questions either in writing or as responses to an interview conducted by someone else.

☐☐ **Internal—external control questionnaire**
  1 Make a list of some of the most important and valued features of your present life. These might be family relationships or friendships, interests and satisfactions at work, cultural or physical activities . . . In what ways would your life change for the worse if you lost any of the items on your list?

2 Consider the item you hold nearest and dearest and estimate the likelihood of losing it in the near future:

highly
unlikely   unlikely   possible   likely   highly
                                                      likely

3 What are the things that would

(a) contribute to your continued possession of this item?
(b) cause you to lose it?

4 What do you most look forward to in your own life?
5 Why is it important to you?
6 How likely is it that you will get what you hope for?

highly
unlikely   unlikely   possibly   likely   highly
                                                      likely

7 If you were to succeed in this ambition, what would be the most important cause of that?
8 If you were to fail, why would that be?
9 How important would it be to you to know how far you were personally responsible for succeeding or failing in achieving your aims/hopes?

The results of this interview, which can be written down, or recorded on audio-tape, can be interpreted in a fairly straightforward fashion. Fatalists are likely to feel little or no control over the major events in their lives, and to see what happens to them as the product of external forces. People with a strong sense of control over their own destinies are more likely to stress the part they can personally play in bringing about change and sustaining certain features of their lives. It should not be assumed that helpers will automatically find themselves towards the self-controlling end of the spectrum, but a helper with an unremittingly fatalistic view of life's twists and turns would be something of a contradiction in terms.

Discuss the findings either with the person who conducted the interview or with someone else. If two or three pairs of individuals have interviewed each other, a group discussion would be fruitful.

Other views about the outside world and the people in it can take the form of theories, or subscriptions to bodies of organized belief. Most people do not, however, have a neat set of theoretical propositions inside their heads; they tend to collect bits and pieces from here and there, sometimes from incompatible and contradictory sources, which they shape into a rough working philosophy which they never, or hardly ever have to articulate to themselves, or make public all at once. Hence the survival in many such schemes of mutually inconsistent ideas about the world. The ideas can, however, be grouped roughly into a number of categories.

Social and political theories identify the causes of the ills of the world in social, political, and economic structures, and the remedies to them in social and political action. For example, 'What's wrong with the world today is that a few people push the rest of us about'; 'People are too envious of the achievements of successful people'; 'Crime is caused by advertising'; 'Poverty can be abolished'; 'Education acts against the interests of the working class'.

Psychological theories tend to be of two kinds, the psychodynamic (e.g. 'People are depressed because they can't have stable and satisfying personal relationships'; 'Early experiences are vital in shaping the adult personality'; 'The capacity to trust other human beings is sadly absent from contemporary family life') and the behaviourist (e.g. 'All behaviour is learned behaviour and it can be changed by manipulating the rewards and punishments it attracts').

Religious beliefs vary according to t⟨ ⟩enets of the major faiths, and to sectarian positions within them, but they tend to agree on the subordination of mankind to the greater purposes of a divinity whose revealed word includes a moral code for the ordering of life in this world.

Common-sense theories. A great many people also subscribe to 'common-sense' versions of what once were highly specialized and 'scientific' theories. They consist of assertions about declining standards of behaviour; poor parental control of children; the impact of the mass media and of American 'culture' on young people, and on moral standards; of the deleterious effects of working mothers; of high-rise flats; of laziness and obtuseness in the labour force; of the corroding effects of greed and envy, etc. The other side of this negative coin is to be found in recipes for action that stress the removal of corrupting influences and the restoration of more vigorous correctional methods in place of the debilitating effects of permissive and non-punitive 'treatments'.

These are not, of course, the only categories that can be applied to personal values, nor do the comments under each heading do justice to their richness and complexity.

☐☐ Try using these categories, plus any others which appear interesting or important, to classify the statements you made in response to the three exercises above. Is it possible to characterize your views as belonging mainly to one or other of them? Do they cross over several categories? Or belong to none of them? What label would you put on your own position or positions? To what extent are they shared or opposed by your colleagues at work? What would the people you try to help think of them? Are they recognizable in the work you do, or masked in some way? Which of them would you communicate to colleagues or customers? How long have you held these views? What were the important influences in your holding them? Have any of them changed? When and why?

☐☐ Another way of exploring what the word 'help' means to you is to write a brief history of the occasions in your own life when you have requested help from others.

Your attitude as someone who is going to *give* help to others might well be influenced by what happened at those times in the past when you were a *recipient* of it.

Try making a list of as many as possible of the instances in which you have asked another person for help. Examining each situation in turn, see if you can answer some questions such as: What was the problem I was faced with at the time? Whom did I ask for help? What sort of response did I receive? What kind of help was I given and how valuable was it? What if anything can I learn from this encounter? How would I respond to someone who approached me with a similar problem?

When you have done this for a few occurrences from your own experience, you can then review them together to see whether any patterns emerge. For example, do you typically ask others for help with a certain kind of problem? Do you always ask the same people? Have the kinds of things with which you have asked for help changed at different stages in your life? If possible, compare your history with that of a colleague or friend and look for similarities and differences.

☐☐ Dilemmas

Values and preferences often lie dormant until circumstances force people to take one side or the other in an argument or dispute — should you join the Roundheads or the Cavaliers as the Civil War sweeps towards you? Here are four dilemmas of the kind which confront helpers. What would your responses be?

☐ Racism

You are working on the street with a group of unemployed teenagers; boys and girls; all of them white but living in a run-down inner city area near substantial West Indian and Asian communities. One or two of the more forceful members of the group have very strong views about immigrants, which they express in offensive racist language. Most of the other members do not make such comments but laugh or show approval when they are made by the dominant group members. Would you say anything about it and, if so, what?

☐ Confidentiality

You are attempting to help a very disturbed and disruptive girl of fifteen. After many failures you eventually win her confidence; or appear to. During a casual conversation she implies, but does not say outright, that she has been having sex with a seventeen-year-old boy who has left the school. What do you do?

☐ Suicide

In your capacity as a voluntary worker at a rehabilitation unit you are talking to a man of twenty-four, previously a promising athlete who is paralysed from the waist down as a result of a car accident two years ago. He also has facial injuries, and suffers from severe migraines which cannot be effectively controlled by medication. He has broken off his engagement and tells you that he is determined to commit suicide. He asks for your help in achieving this; saying that he will do it anyway, whether you agree or not, and that by not helping him you make it likely that his death will be more difficult and painful than it would be otherwise. What do you say to him?

☐ Contraception

In a recent shuffle of cases a colleague has taken over responsibility for Cynthia, a young woman of low intelligence whose four-year-old daughter is already in long-term care following proceedings for neglect and physical abuse by Cynthia and her former boy-friend.

Cynthia is pregnant again, by another man, and asks your colleague to help arrange an abortion because she is afraid that the same thing will happen to a new baby. Your colleague has strong anti-abortion views and counsels Cynthia to have the baby and have it adopted. You think that Cynthia will want to keep the baby if it is born. You meet her in the street one day and she asks for your advice. What do you tell her?

Look at your responses to these four dilemmas. How did you decide what to do? By reference to a deeply held value or belief? Or to some sliding scale of situational contingencies? Instantly — or after some thought? Discuss your reactions with others who have looked at the same dilemmas and compare results. It is unlikely that there will be complete agreement on how to deal with these and similarly intractable problems.

Here are some briefer exercises for defining and refining some of your attitudes and values:

☐ Private member's bill

You have won the annual ballot for a private member's bill to be presented to Parliament. What would be the subject and main provisions of the bill you would present?

☐ Advertisements

— Write a small display advertisement to put in your local newspaper announcing the services of your agency to local people.
— Write an advertisement for yourself, as though you were setting up in business as an independent helper, telling prospective customers what you are offering. Emphasize any special interests, skill, or experience that you have and characterize your general working style.

☐ Sacking issues

Imagine that you are the head of a small social work agency. You have to produce a document which defines cases of professional misconduct for which members of staff can expect to be dismissed. What kinds of behaviour will you include, and why?

☐ **Resigning issues**
- Imagine that the helping agency where you work has been taken over by a new management team with totally different views about social work to your own, which it means to put into practice. Under what circumstances would you feel compelled to resign?
- Under *present* working conditions can you think of any circumstances in which you would feel that you had to resign rather than do as you were told by senior management? What would they be?

☐ **Professional ethics**
Working in a small group — four to six persons — constitute yourselves as a professional ethics committee for the job that you do: social worker, teacher, counsellor, adviser, residential worker, probation officer. Your task is to devise a code of conduct for the members of your occupation. Limit yourself to ten statements or propositions, and try to make at least a proportion of them positive ones rather than making them all negative.

☐ **A personal statement**
Whatever your views, or assumptions or values, the best way to make them clear to yourself is to make a statement of them, as succinctly as you can, and on one side of a sheet of paper if possible. They can be cast in the form of a personal 'ten commandments' or in a more general form. Would you be happy to show them to colleagues at work, to friends, to the people who make use of your service?

☐☐ **Helping and responsibility**
A factor which influences many people's willingness to help others with their problems is the extent to which they believe individuals are themselves responsible for the predicaments they are in. 'You got yourself into it, now you can get yourself out of it.' The plight of many who have broken the law or who have in some other way deviated from the norms of society is seen by a large number of people as justly deserved. The earthquake victim calls forth our unreserved sympathy; but someone who deliberately sets fire to their own home will be much less likely to receive our compassion even though their consequent misfortunes are largely the same. In most circumstances it is far less easy to apportion the causes of people's problems between their own actions and external forces acting upon them.

Look at the list of people in the box and try to decide whether you would be willing to help them with their problems. If you would not assist some of them, or would do so only reluctantly, make a list of the reasons why you feel this way. What do your reactions tell you about your general attitude to helping? Can you draw a dividing line between those whom you would be happy to help and those whom you would reject or be hesitant to help? Does this line signify anything about your underlying values?

— An old-age pensioner with substantial money problems.
— A child suffering from polio.
— A mother of three (married) suffering from depression.
— A mother of three (unmarried) suffering from depression.
— A mother of three, suffering from depression, who has assaulted one of her children.
— An alcoholic tramp who frequently asks you for money.
— A thirty-year-old man who has convictions for molesting small children.
— A teenage girl who has made 'attention-seeking' suicide attempts on four previous occasions.
— An unemployed father of two children whose wife works, who says he wants a job but who doesn't seem to try very hard to find one.
— A teenage boy who is in trouble for hooliganism at football matches.
— An ex-public schoolboy, from a well-off family, who asks for help with money problems.
— A man suffering from depression following a serious motor accident which he had caused through drunkenness.

☐☐ Contesting values

As a final test of some of the ideas you have uncovered during these exercises, invite a friend or colleague to attack them. He/she should act the devil's advocate with as much logic and vigour as is compatible with your continuing friendship or working relationship. This works best if your adversary has had some time to study a written statement of your values or beliefs and has prepared a searching assault on your positions. Repeating the process in reverse allows you to get some of your own back.

Notes and references

The definition of the social worker's task at the beginning of the chapter is taken from the *Classification of Occupations and Directory of Occupational Titles* (CODOT) published by Her Majesty's Stationery Office. A more detailed description of what social workers actually do is given in P. Parsloe (1981) *Social Services Area Teams* (London: Allen and Unwin). Guidance on writing job descriptions can be obtained from M. Turrell (1980) *Training Analysis* (Plymouth: Macdonald and Evans). And a more educationally oriented guide is R. F. Mager and P. Pipe (1970) *Analyzing Performance Problems* (Belmont, Cal.: Fearon Publishers).

For a good general introduction to the whole area of values and behaviour, see Derek Wright (1971) *The Psychology of Moral Behaviour* (Harmondsworth: Penguin). A large number of exercises for critically examining your own values is to be found in S. Simon, L. Howe, and H. Kirschenbaum (1972) *Values Clarification* (New York: Hart). The questionnaire on page 10 follows closely the one developed by H. Lefcourt (1976) *Locus of Control* (Hillsdale, N.J.: Lawrence Erlbaum), who is in turn adapting the work of J. B. Rotter (1966) Generalized Expectancies for Internal versus External Control of Reinforcement. *Psychological Monographs* 80 (whole no. 609).

3 Interviewing

The first step in most helping encounters is almost always some form of assessment interview. Some encounters begin and end in fact with a single interview during which assistance or advice is given, even if it is nothing more than referral to the services of another agency. Others act as a gateway to a variety of possible paths through the maze of welfare and social work provision. Initial interviews therefore, like Janus, face both ways – *outwards* from the agency as a sort of shop window through which people can see, sometimes only dimly, what is on offer and what they are letting themselves in for – and *inwards* by assessing and pointing the newcomer in roughly the right direction.

Interviewing is also important because it forms the basis of many other helping efforts, like giving advice, counselling, and group discussion. But one of the difficulties of doing something about improving the skills of interviewing is that talking to other people is the most important medium through which ordinary social relationships of all sorts are conducted, from the most distant and formal to the most intimate and loving. It is not easy in many situations to mark off a precise point at which casual conversation ceases and interviewing as such begins. This lack of precision can lead to two related conclusions: one is a denial that interviewing constitutes a proper subject of study at all, and the other is a failure to recognize the nature and importance of the skills which make for *effective* interviewing. So the first need is for a definition of interviewing which helps to distinguish it from everyday discourse.

> FOR THE PURPOSE OF THIS CHAPTER AN INTERVIEW IS A FORMAL CONVERSATION IN WHICH A HELPER (TYPICALLY THE EMPLOYEE OF AN OFFICIAL OR SEMI-OFFICIAL AGENCY) SEEKS INFORMATION FROM SOMEONE IN NEED OF HELP.

An interview differs from ordinary conversation first by virtue of its purpose, and second by the distinctions that are normally made between the specific roles of the participants. The purposes may be of many kinds, for example assessment, fact finding, selection, but in a good interview it is important that whatever they are they are made clear to both parties from the outset. Differences of role are usually much more obvious, part of the furniture of the occasion, since the interviewer tends to be an official of a social work or voluntary agency, and the person being interviewed is typically an applicant or supplicant in search of a service or benefit of some kind.

These distinctions are usually reflected in the proportion of time that the participants spend actually talking in an interview. Unlike ordinary conversation between friends, where something like fifty-fifty might be normal, in a formal interview the interviewer tends to speak for very much less of the available time than the person being interviewed – a ratio of 4:1 or even 9:1 would not be unusual, the exact proportion varying according to the nature of the topic under discussion, the characteristics of the person being interviewed, and the personal style of the interviewer. As to the *quality* of the contributions which interviewers make to the proceedings, any discussion of them runs the risk either of being trite and obvious on the one hand or of pretentious theorizing on the other. We shall try to steer a middle course between these twin pitfalls in this chapter, which starts with some simple ways of looking at what actually goes on in interviews and making some estimate of personal competence.

The major part of the chapter is devoted to tracing the course of the interview and breaking it down into some of its component parts: defining aims; planning the form and content of the encounter; asking questions to elicit information; using appropriate non-verbal communication; and finally summarizing what has been said. The chapter ends with some suggestions for improving interview skills, building on the self-awareness promoted by earlier exercises, and using systematic feedback to get better at talking to other people, finding out facts, and coping with some of the problems that sometimes confront even the most skilful interviewer.

Assessing skills

It is virtually impossible to survive into adulthood in our kind of society without gaining *some* experience of interviewing. So although people may never have held paid positions as interviewers, they will almost certainly have been interviewed themselves at school, or for a training course, or job, or by officials of one or another of the multifarious agencies which mediate the care and concern professed by modern states for their citizens. It is also unlikely that helpers of any description will have escaped the need to ask people questions. The first few exercises of this chapter provide opportunities to review these experiences before looking in more detail at the specifics of interviewing itself.

☐☐ **Record of interview experience and training**

The aim of this exercise is to help you define in some detail your past experience of interviewing, and of any training you have had for it, and of any other skills, attributes, or experiences which are of use to you in this activity.

NAME _____ AGE _____

PRESENT JOB _____

PREVIOUS JOBS _____

_____

How long have you been interviewing other people? _____ yrs.

☐   How many interviews do you conduct in a typical week/typical year?

☐   How many interviews have you completed in your entire career as an

interviewer? Estimate _____

Here is a list of common kinds of interview, with spaces in which you can indicate whether you have had experience of them, on either side of the table:

Experience as Interviewer	TYPE OF INTERVIEW	Experience as Interviewee
_____	Assessment	_____
_____	Intake	_____
_____	Selection	_____
_____	Fact Finding	_____
_____	Market Research	_____
_____	Disciplinary	_____
_____	Research	_____
_____	Monitoring	_____

List the categories of people that you have interviewed.

_____   _____

_____   _____

_____   _____

Any other relevant experience   _____

_____

Previous training in interviewing:

_____   None

_____   Watching others

_____   Instruction

_____   Demonstration

_____   Skills practice with systematic feedback experience

Tick those which apply to you.

Any other relevant training   _____

_____

What are your strengths as an interviewer?   _____

_____

_____

What are your weaknesses as an interviewer?   _____

_____

_____

Are there any categories of people you find difficult to interview?   _____

_____

_____

☐ Work with someone else to expand and elaborate on the topics suggested in this brief survey. Find out more about your partner's experience of interviewing, about the parts he/she enjoys or dislikes, and about strengths and weaknesses.

Speech rate sampling

The most basic measurement that can be made of behaviour in the interview is the relative amount of time that each party spends talking. There are no real rules of thumb for deciding what the correct proportions should be in any particular instance but, within limits, the less the interviewer says the better. The most precise way of determining this ratio in practice is by observation and analysis. This can be done *in vivo* by an observer using a simple recording sheet, or it can be done in retrospect by the interviewer, using audio or video tape-recorded dialogue.

In either case, *all* the contributions of the participants can be individually timed, noted down, and totalled; a lengthy and somewhat tedious process. A more economical method is to note at exact ten-second intervals who happens to be talking at that moment:

Speech samples: ten-second intervals

Interviewer	Interviewee
⊦⊦⊦⊦ ١	⊦⊦⊦⊦￢ ⊦⊦⊦⊦￢ ⊦⊦⊦⊦￢ ⊦⊦⊦⊦￢ ⊦⊦⊦⊦￢ ١١ ١١
Total = 6 (20%)	Total = 24 (80%)

In this example, the interviewer was talking on six of the ten-second points during a five-minute interview and the interviewee occupied the remaining twenty-four.

In order to arrive at a reasonably accurate picture of your own technique you would need to repeat this scoring procedure on a number of occasions, and to distinguish carefully between different kinds of interview; also making some allowance for the nature of the person being interviewed, who may tend towards the talkative or the silent ends of the spectrum. If you appear to be talking too much of the time, practise saying less, asking shorter questions, listening for longer, etc.

Critical incidents

One way of assessing skills is to describe a *critical incident* when something either went badly wrong, or was highly successful, because of something that you did or did not do, in this case during an interview. Since the aim at this point is to identify aspects of interviewing skill which require improvement, we will focus particularly on an occasion when things did not go well. This can be done initially by simply thinking about the incident and recreating it in the mind's eye as it were. Or it can be done with the assistance of others by writing out or dictating some of the dialogue and attempting to reconstruct the events as a role-played *action replay*:

Some points to bear in mind
— Who was involved in the incident – the *dramatis personae*; brief descriptions of them would be useful.
— What was the occasion of the interview or assessment session?
— When did the critical incident occur in the encounter?
— How had things been going until then?
— What actually happened, including verbatim reports on what was said by both parties to the interview?
— How did you feel when the critical bit happened?
— What effect did it have on the person being interviewed?
— How did you try to cope with it? Was it successful?
— Why do you think it happened?
— Could it have been avoided?
— What skills, awareness, sensitivity did you lack in that situation?
— How would you cope with it if a similar situation arose now?

The creative process of directing other people in the key roles of the incident and perhaps recording the finished product on videotape can highlight hitherto unsuspected aspects of the debacle. The point of the exercise, however, is not to furnish cheap entertainment for fellow learners at your expense, but to pinpoint ways of dealing better with that kind of situation in the future.

☐☐ Interview skills check-list
How good are you at doing the following things? Put a ring around the number which is nearest to where you think you are on each of these scales.

	Very good				Not very good
1 Planning an interview; deciding on what needs to be covered, and in what order.	5	4	3	2	1
2 Explaining the purpose of an interview in a way that is clearly understood.	5	4	3	2	1
3 Forming realistic impressions of someone from appearance, dress, speech, and mannerisms.	5	4	3	2	1

	Very good				Not very good
4 Asking questions in a clear and concise way.	5	4	3	2	1
5 Encouraging the interviewee to talk freely.	5	4	3	2	1
6 Coping with a silent or withdrawn individual.	5	4	3	2	1
7 Coping with someone who talks too much, or about irrelevant matters.	5	4	3	2	1
8 Assessing the mood of the person being interviewed.	5	4	3	2	1
9 Summarizing what has emerged from an interview accurately and acceptably.	5	4	3	2	1
10 Concluding an interview on a positive note.	5	4	3	2	1

Scores in the '1' or '2' columns indicate skills to which some time and training effort could usefully be devoted. High scores, on the other hand, do not necessarily mean that there is nothing to be learned in those areas. In order to secure some comparison with your own judgement of your performance, ask someone who has seen you at work to complete the same ratings. If there are points of disagreement between you, a third person can be brought in to adjudicate. But remember that all judgements of this nature, no matter who makes them, are no more than *indications* – they do not by themselves constitute *proof* as to the quality of your work, one way or the other.

The parts of the interview

A not uncommon way of learning how to interview is to jump in at the deep end and leave the rest to experience – sometimes of the painful variety. The end product is often a perfectly serviceable technique, but the aim of this chapter is to present some short cuts to the same destination by making the whole process *explicit* rather than *implicit*, and therefore more under the control of the learner. The interview itself is an episode of behaviour that has a beginning, a middle, and an end, accompanied (normally) by an unacknowledged orchestration of non-verbal elements. In the exercises below we follow the progress of the interview from beginning to end and look separately at some of the ingredients in that elusive mix that marks the performance of a skilful interviewer.

▢▢ Defining the aims

The first step in preparing for a successful interview is to make a clear statement of its purpose. Imagine that you are a personnel officer about to interview a candidate for a job with your firm/organization. Write down what the aim of the meeting will be:

The purpose of this interview is to _____

_____

_____

This aim may be simple or complex, easy to communicate or more difficult. Some things to look for in your definition:

Does it stress	*For example*
THE ORGANIZATION?	The purpose of this interview is to select the right person for this job.
THE INTERVIEWER?	. . . to find out whether I could work with this person.
THE INTERVIEWEE?	. . . to find the best job possible for this applicant.

A single definition could embrace each of these three dimensions, and others besides, but if an emphasis has been placed on one rather than another it may indicate something about the personal style and inclination of the interviewer.

☐ Select *three* different types of interview you may be called on to undertake in your helping work. Formulate a direct and simple definition of aims for each interview.

☐ Discuss and review these aims with a partner to see how clear they are and whether they could be improved.

☐ Incorporate each of the aims in separate letters making appointments with the people you propose to interview. Will it be clear to the recipients why they are being invited to see you? If not, rewrite the letters until it *is* clear.

Structuring the interview

To the novice, the most impressive feature of a skilfully conducted interview is the apparent ease with which the dialogue flows naturally from one topic to another until all the relevant areas have been covered, leaving no gaps or omissions, and all with no sense of strain or interrogation. But because the performance has the outward appearance of a seamless garment, it may be difficult to see how or where to begin to do likewise.

The secret often lies in the *structure* of the interview, the result in some cases of conscious planning on the part of the interviewer, for others the product of long experience and the self-confidence that comes from competent past performance. It is conventional to distinguish three degrees of structure in interviews:

1 *Structured:* in which every topic is defined in advance. In the case of some types of market and other research interviews, the actual form of words for each question has been formulated by the designer of the particular schedule. This has the virtue,

for research purposes, of ensuring that all the subjects are responding to exactly the same words. For most helping purposes, however, such exactitude is not necessary, except for identifying data such as *name, age, address,* etc.

2 *Semi-structured:* a mixture of pre-prepared topics and precise questions with more 'open-ended' questions which allow the person being interviewed more latitude in his or her replies. A typical assessment interview would take a semi-structured form.

3 *Unstructured:* sometimes seen as the pinnacle of professional endeavour in interviewing technique. It has no formal structure, no predetermined parameters, no precise forms of words. The interviewer has no agenda beyond the expressed interests and concerns of the person being interviewed. So the end product should be a more or less faithful reflection of the interviewee's interests expressed in personal terms. This is the opposite of what happens in the structured interview, where the respondent's replies are fitted into a preordained framework. An unstructured interview might be used in market or social research to throw up possible leads for later enquiry of a more exact nature, or in social work to break out of a log jam by suggesting fresh avenues of approach to particularly knotty problems.

Two types of questions

The most commonly drawn distinction between different kinds of questions to ask in interviews is that of 'closed' versus 'open-ended'. *Closed* questions ask for specific pieces of information, like How old are you? When did this first happen? Are you married? Have you ever had anything wrong with your heart before? Are you working at the moment? The *open-ended* question on the other hand is one that does not predict its own reply, or confine it too narrowly. It cannot usually be answered with a single word, a 'yes' or a 'no', or a piece of information. For example, Can you tell me something about yourself? How did you get into this position? What sorts of things do you really dislike about this? Can you start at the beginning and go on from there? What's on your mind? Can I help you? How are you feeling now? With experience, interviewers soon acquire a stock of both sorts of questions which serve for most situations; the wider and more adaptable the stock, the more flexible the technique they permit.

☐☐ Specify an interview topic and make two lists of questions related to it; one list of 'closed' questions to elicit hard facts, the other 'open-ended' to explore matters further in the language of the respondent.

Writing an interview plan

Experienced interviewers work to plans and strategies which have long since ceased to be conscious entities; beginners will find it useful to write out some headings and some questions. Both of these will depend on the purpose and nature of the interview, but using the distinction just made between 'open' and 'closed' questions, let's start with the gathering of basic information:

APPLICATION FOR A HIRE PURCHASE LOAN	Possible questions
Name _____ Mr, Mrs, Ms, Miss	Can you give me your full name, please? Is that Miss, Mrs, Ms?
Age _____	How old are you now?
Address _____ _____ _____	What is your full address?
Occupation _____ Length of time in current job _____ yrs Average weekly wage £_____ Major outgoings/per week £	What job do you do? Can you tell me your occupation? What is your average take-home pay?
Rent _____ Fuel _____ HP _____ . . . . _____ . . . . _____	

Questions like these fall firmly at the *structured* end of the continuum; asking them and recording the answers in the spaces provided does not require too much time or skill. More of both commodities are needed to plan and execute a *semi-structured* interview in which a mixture of types of information is gathered: 'hard' data that could be computerized, like the responses to the loan application form; 'softer' facts about experience, attitudes, and behaviour which are less easy to elicit and record; and a background 'noise' of barely perceptible impressions and feelings picked up through a variety of channels.

Items for interviews of this sort should be thought about in advance and laid out in some logical way, either in writing or in your head as a mental prompt list. If you were considering an applicant for an alcoholic rehabilitation scheme with a strictly limited number of places, an outline interview plan might look like this:

Alcoholic rehabilitation scheme: intake interview plan
Personal details
— age
— address
— occupation (if any)
— marital situation

Drinking history
— onset
— patterns
— effects

Current situation
— dried out?
— on medication?
— relations with relations/friends
— health
— work prospects

Motivation
— evidence of willingness to do something
— reasons for wishing to change
— why is it different this time?
— previous treatment
— future plans
— previous attempts
— honesty

Knowledge of scheme
— does applicant know what you are trying to do?

Under each of the items listed in the plan it would be possible to ask a number of specific questions, for example:

Reasons for wishing to change
Can you tell me something about why you are applying for this unit?
Do you know anyone who's been here?
What will happen to you if you don't get a place in the scheme?
What's the biggest obstacle in the way of your staying dry?
What can you offer to other people attending the unit?
Why should we take you rather than someone else?

What's the longest time you would be willing to wait for a place?
Are your friends/relatives/loved ones prepared to help you?

☐ Write out outline interview plans for the following:

(a) Selecting young people for a community service scheme decorating old peoples' homes.
(b) Choosing a staff member to work with you.
(c) A pre-discharge interview with a psychiatric patient in a hospital.
(d) A preliminary interview with a non-school-attending girl.

☐ Now think of four likely interviews for use in your own work situation and write out plans for them.

☐ Discuss your interview plans with one or more colleagues; they should add categories where necessary and suggest further questions that could be asked.

Devising specific questions

If inspiration alone fails to yield a sufficient number of questions to ask under different topic heads, try using the '5 W-H' method:

WHO WHAT WHERE WHEN WHY and HOW

Who are you? Who else is affected by this problem? Who can tell me more about you? Who has helped you in the past? Who has harmed your interests?

What exactly is the problem? What is bothering you? What can you tell me about this? What has gone wrong? What is happening to you? What do you want me to do?

Where do you come from? Where do you find this happens? Where is the pain? Where are your parents? Where have you lived in the past? Where can I come to see you? Where do you work? Where are you thinking of going later on?

When did this first happen? When did you first notice something wrong? When do you normally have these difficulties? When did you leave home? When did you start work there? When did you first realize that you were different from other people?

Why have you come to see me? Why do you always get into this sort of trouble? Why didn't you think of doing something earlier? Why don't you get more help from your relatives? Why do you think you do it? Why are you so unhappy?

How did you get into this mess? How can I help you? How did you hear of this service? How have you managed for so long? How old are you? How long have you been in this position? How strongly do you feel about that? How anxious do your parents feel?

The quantity of questions that can be generated using these six words is almost limitless, but will be constrained in practice by the specific purpose of the interview, by the time available, and by the capacity of the person being interviewed to make useful replies. Another way of using the '5 W-H' system to get even more leverage on a subject area is to divide possible questions into more than one category, for example:

Topic: depressive feelings

	things associated with onset of depression	*things associated with alleviation of depression*
WHO	who makes you feel depressed?	who makes you feel better?
WHAT	what events seem to predate the onset of bad feelings?	what activities make you feel better?
WHERE	where do you feel worst?	where can you go to lift your spirits?
WHEN	when is the worst time of the day	. . .
WHY	. . .	
HOW	. . .	

☐ Use the '5 W-H' device to generate lists of questions for an interview topic of your own choosing.

☐ Develop at least two columns of '5 W-H' questions for another topic.

☐ Divide a group into six 'teams', each of which might be an individual but preferably with three or four members. Allocate one 'W' word and the 'H' word to different groups and announce a competition for generating questions on the theme of 'Unemployment' or any other relevant topic, the winner being the group that writes the largest number of them on a large sheet within a specified period — say five minutes. This normally leads to upwards of 70–80 questions in no time at all. Display the results on a wall.

'I couldn't ask that'

Despite the structured role of the interviewer and the formal nature of the function in many official agencies, it often proves impossible to disavow a lifetime's learning and habits in relation to different kinds of people, and the ways in which they can be spoken to, and on what subjects.

□□ The following table plots some types of people against some areas of questioning. Rate how *comfortable* you would feel asking questions about those topics for each kind of person; using the following scale:

1 Very comfortable
2 Quite comfortable
3 Neither comfortable nor uncomfortable
4 Slightly uncomfortable
5 Very uncomfortable

Kinds of people	Questions about												
	Money	Class	Sex	Violence	Family life	Race	Morality	Religion	Work	Feelings	Health	Age	Politics
Same sex													
Opposite sex													
Older than self													
Younger than self													
Higher social class													
Lower social class													
Rich													
Poor													
Unknown													
Social acquaintance													
Friend													
Own relative													
Shy													
Extrovert													
Aggressive													
Ethnic minority													

☐ Make a list of the kinds of people *you* might have difficulties with.

☐ Make a list of some topic areas you might find difficult to broach with some kinds of people.

☐ Take a topic such as *money* or *sex* and formulate some questions as you might be prepared to ask them of different people in the matrix above or in your own list. You would, for example, use different language when talking to young people than to those who are older.

Starting the interview

A good interview starts with an introduction that makes clear the identity and occupation of the interviewer, expresses in simple terms the purpose of the interview, and outlines the conditions under which it is to be conducted; that is what kind of information is being sought and the uses to which it will be put, who will have access to it, and so on. Sometimes this has to be done under less than ideal conditions.

☐☐ Here are four situations in which you have to introduce both yourself and the purpose of the interview; take three or four minutes to prepare what you are going to say, and then try it out on a colleague:

☐ Situation 1
You are an education welfare officer and you call on the parents of a teenage girl to discuss their daughter's poor attendance. They appear not to know that the girl has been absent from school.

☐ Situation 2
You are the counsellor in a voluntary family planning clinic. It is the policy of the clinic to perform sterilizations *only* with the consent of the husband or partner of women who apply for the operation. The wife of a serving prisoner wishes to be sterilized. They have been separated for some time and there is no love lost between them. You have to see him in the prison where he is serving his sentence to ask his consent. How would you start?

☐ Situation 3
As a probation officer you are preparing a social enquiry report for the court on an elderly lady shoplifter. You are visiting her home where you must first of all break the news of the offence to her unsuspecting son and daughter-in-law and explain about the report and the court proceedings.

☐ Situation 4
You are a contact tracer in a special clinic. You ring up a woman to tell her that

she has been named by a male patient and that she may have contracted gonorrhoea from him. You ring her at her office.

☐ Try these situations in pairs, taking turns to introduce the interviews, and discussing at the end of the exercise how things went. The person on the receiving end can report on how it felt and how well the worker did.

☐ If four people work together, each person introduces an interview to one of the others, the remaining two acting as observers who provide feedback.

☐ Identify similar situations which occur in your own work and try out introductions to them.

Forming impressions

Whenever you meet a stranger, you almost immediately form an impression of him or her. In most cases, this may be revised as you talk to the person and get to know him or her better, but the initial impact has an important effect on your behaviour for the first few minutes of the encounter. There are many 'cues' that we use to form these impressions – size and shape, voice, social behaviour, and dress, to name just a few. Our impressions are also influenced by our own previous experiences with other people who look like the stranger. Understanding how we form impressions of others – and awareness of the impressions they may be forming of us – has an important part to play in helping us to improve our dealings with people, especially if we are to give them help in a positive and constructive way.

☐☐ Form a pair with someone you have recently met. Each of you has to make some guesses about the other, based on the 'first impressions' you have formed on the basis of a brief acquaintance. See if you can guess accurately some of the following about the person you are working with.

— Age to within five years (or closer)
— Marital status
— Whether or not he/she has children
— One previous job
— Kind of car
— A favourite pastime
— A favourite television or radio programme
— The kind of music or food this person likes

When you have made all your guesses, go through the list with the person and see how many answers each of you got right about the other. You could then talk about the reasons why you gave various answers and see whether this tells you anything about yourself (the basis on which you make judgements about others). You might also think about the reasons why the other person was right or wrong about you on particular items in the list.

Learning from a skilled interviewer

One of the best ways to improve interview skills is to observe and learn from someone who is good at interviewing. Sometimes this can be arranged with an experienced worker, but often it is not possible to do this easily. Another way of learning how to be better at interviews is to capitalize on the experience and strengths that reside in any group of helpers and would-be helpers whether they are in formal education or not. By observing and commenting on each other's performance, a great deal can be learned in quite a short time.

'Modelling' is a social skills term which simply means observing the behaviour of someone else, usually a more skilled person, and then attempting to reproduce what he/she has done. For example:

☐☐ Introducing an interview

Set a task for introducing an interview. This could be:

— Taking an assessment history for an elderly person.
— Seeking a place in an old people's home.
— Interviewing prospective foster-parents.
— Assessing a child for a place on an adventure scheme.

Allow five minutes for preparing suitable introductory words for such an interview, and then have everyone try out the *spiel* on the person next to him/her so that everyone else can hear. At this level the exercise provides a series of impressions in each observer's head of ways of performing the same task, suitable words to use, expressions to adopt, places to smile. . . .

The exercise can be built on by giving each person in the group a different task, which, after preparation, is presented to everyone else. Discussion follows, and where it appears either to the observers or to the presenter that there are defects in the introduction or that it could be improved in some way, other participants demonstrate how they would do that particular introduction. This may be specially useful in cases where the subject of the interview is a somewhat sticky one as in the exercise on page 32.

Non-verbal communication

Whole books have been devoted to the subtleties of non-verbal communication – nvc to its enthusiasts – and even to smaller parts of the field, like body posture – or 'body language' to the initiated. Gaze, expression, posture, gesture: these are all important parts of the total communications picture, but their importance in isolation should not be overrated. There are research findings which show that some people are more effective at using non-verbal communication than others, and this can have positive effects on the work they do with other people. But there is also a good deal of evidence that science cannot as yet measure in any reliable fashion more than a few of the variables at work in the simplest examples of human interaction. There are individuals for example who break, or at least do not appear to observe, nearly all of the 'rules' of non-verbal communication and still manage to work extremely well with others; carry out good interviews, help people solve their problems, feel better about themselves, achieve insight, and so on. So doing what comes naturally is good advice for anybody in the helping business. On the other hand, your interview behaviour may conform to most of what the non-verbal communication manuals prescribe, and still be marred by an unfortunate mannerism or two of which you may not be aware.

A full-scale analysis of nvc in even a very brief interview could take an enormous amount of time and effort, and the pay-offs might not merit such an expenditure. But a more modest outlay could be repaid with useful insights.

☐ **Mimicry**
This is a simple but effective way of getting instant feedback on some of the non-verbal elements in your repertoire. Set up an interview on any topic with a friend or colleague; a third person sits behind the interviewee's chair and mimics your posture, gestures, and facial expressions. You might find this disconcerting at first, not to say hilarious, but the purpose of the exercise is serious enough. It is to give you continuous information about what you are doing. When the inevitable sensations of self-consciousness have evaporated, you will be able to use this flesh-and-blood mirror to assess the appropriateness or otherwise of some of your non-verbal communications and to modify them in ways you may think desirable.

☐ **'Faces'**
A variation on the theme of instant feedback is to replace the live face and features of a colleague with stylized expressions drawn on pieces of card the size of dinner plates, which can be displayed as appropriate during a practice interview:

Whenever the interviewer smiles, the observer holds up the smiling face; when the interviewer is not smiling, the observer holds up the non-smiling face. Besides providing feedback of a neutral kind, this exercise can also incorporate a gentle reinforcement of smiling behaviour if that is thought desirable. (In the case of slightly immature personalities it may also result initially in fits of uncontrollable giggles.)

Listening skills

Listening is not just a passive event, it consists of active and visible behaviours which are directly signalled to the person who is doing the talking. If the signals fail to appear in the first place, or, having appeared, then disappear, the effect on the speaker can be disconcerting to say the least. Professional interviewers, and especially some of those who appear on television, display an exaggerated version of active listening behaviour – all smiles and nods and eager attention which would drive away not a few of the people who turn up every day at their local helping agencies. These caricatures do not provide precise models for helpers to follow, but they do point to the importance of listening skills in an interview.

SOME RULES FOR LISTENING

LOOK at the person you are talking to – not too much, which will make him/her feel stared at. Not too little or he/she will feel you are not interested. *Look* at the person when you begin to say something yourself, or for the duration of a brief question. *Look* when the person begins to speak, and as he/she begins to wind up or falter.

SMILE. Not all the time like a Cheshire cat, and not so rarely as a sunny day in November, but enough to show that you are awake and listening, and also what an essentially nice person you are.

NOD. No need to outdo Noddy, but gently affirmative movements of the head will show that you are following the train of an argument and will encourage the speaker to go on speaking.

GRUNT. Not the porcine variety but a sub-verbal form of non-verbal communication, e.g. uh-huh, mmmmmmm. Serves the same purposes as looking, smiling, and nodding, that is, assures the talker of your continued attention and encourages further speech.

USE VERBAL FOLLOWING, PRODS, CUES, AND PROBES. These are words and phrases that signify you have received the message and which prompt the flow a little further: 'I know what you mean. Of course. I see. Yes. Go on. And then . . . Well . . . So? Oh, dear. No! You don't say. What a thing to say! Amazing! Fancy! I know! There you are!'

Finally it is possible to convey listening by the way you sit and compose your limbs; use an alert posture as opposed to one at rest (see p. 74).

☐☐ Non-verbal communication observation schedule

This exercise presents a simple observation schedule for scrutinizing some non-verbal features of your interviewing behaviour; you can use it to analyse your own performance recorded on a video tape recorder, using the schedule during playback to rate your strengths and weaknesses; or, if you do not have access to video equipment, someone else can assist you by watching you at work, and filling in the schedule either at the time or later, and then discussing the results with you.

Name of interviewer _____

Topic of interview _____

Duration of interview _____ minutes.

1. *Gaze*
The amount of time the interviewer spent looking directly at the person being interviewed seemed to be:

Far too little	Not enough	About right	A bit too much	Far too much

Underline the description you agree with.

2. *Expression*
Which of the following expressions did the interviewer use during the interview?

Smile	Sympathetic	Interested
Frown	Inquiring	Bored
Neutral	Questioning	Tired

Which expression was the most common? _____

3. *Voice tone*
Rate the interviewer's voice tone on the following scales:

Always the same ⌊_____|_____|_____|_____⌋ Very varied

Suited to topic ⌊_____|_____|_____|_____⌋ Not suited to topic

4. *Posture*
Was the interviewer's posture:

	YES	NO
Alert	_____	_____
Positive	_____	_____
Neutral	_____	_____
Encouraging	_____	_____

5. *Gesture*
Did the interviewer use appropriate gestures?   YES _____   NO _____
If 'yes' describe them here _____
_____

Did the interviewer use any obvious or irritating mannerisms, e.g. fiddling with face, lips, hair, with paper clips or rubber bands, etc?
If so, what were they? _____
_____
_____

6. *'Following'*
Count the number of times the interviewer (a) nodded, and (b) said 'uh-huh' or made other verbal signals of understanding or agreement:

Number of nods   _____
Number of 'uh-huhs'   _____
Number of minutes in interview_____
Nod rate per minute   _____
'Uh-huh' rate per minute   _____

Finding out the facts

Assessment interviewing consists of finding out as many relevant facts as possible about the person being assessed. Good preparation will increase the likelihood of success but cannot guarantee it. This exercise is designed to provide practice in asking direct fact-finding questions.

☐☐ Two people work together, each of them armed with one of the fact sheets below. Each sheet contains twenty items of information − about a housing applicant, and a hyperactive child. The participants take it in turns to ask questions about one of these two cases for ten minutes at the most. Every time the questioner asks a question which elicits one of the facts on the sheet, the respondent places a tick against it. If questions are asked to which there are no answers, say so. At the end of the two allotted periods compare total scores. Individual interviewers vary in both their work rate and their accuracy, but these particular tasks may not be all that accurate a test of assessment skills due to the unfamiliarity of the topics they use.

   To check on your effectiveness on more familiar ground, you should ask your partner to compile a similar list of items describing a case of the kind you are more likely to encounter in your own helping activities, and see how many you score on that.

Housing applicant

 1 Married – living with wife/husband   _____

 2 Two children   _____

 3 Boy aged six; girl aged four   _____

 4 Present accommodation – two rooms   _____

 5 Rent £20 p.w.   _____

 6 Furnished – poor condition   _____

 7 Share bathroom and toilet   _____

 8 Share kitchen   _____

 9 Damp in rooms   _____

10 Paraffin heater   _____

11 Rats and mice   _____

12 Landlord lives elsewhere   _____

13 You are in work: partner unemployed   _____

14 Earning £80 a week   _____

15 Under threat of redundancy   _____

16 Wife/husband has had bronchitis   _____

17 Son suffers from eczema   _____

18 No savings   _____

19 Been living in these rooms for six months   _____

20 Not on council waiting list   _____

Parent of hyperactive child

 1 Married   _____

 2 Hyperactive child aged twelve   _____

 3 A boy called Robert   _____

 4 Two other children   _____

 5 Twins aged ten   _____

 6 Twin girls   _____

 7 Normal pregnancy with Robert   _____

 8 Slightly difficult birth   _____

    9 Was always an overactive child   _____

10 Wet the bed till age eight   _____

11 Rushes into situations   _____

12 Gets on people's nerves   _____

13 Has no real friends   _____

14 Apparently normal intelligence   _____

15 In remedial class for reading difficulties   _____

16 Father unemployed   _____

17 Mother depressed   _____

18 Robert's behaviour getting worse   _____

19 Tried GP and child guidance   _____

20 Robert not delinquent   _____

Taking a history

The purpose of many assessment interviews is that of 'taking a history'. Although this sounds ambitious – a little like writing a full-scale biography – it usually means picking a slender and highly selective thread through the press of events that crowd the life stories of even the most average individuals. As with any interview, a good place to start is with a clear aim: 'I am taking this history in order to understand how this person came to be in this position/mess/predicament and to see whether, and in what ways, I could do something helpful about it.' An aim like this sets limits to the inquiry but gives little guidance about the specific topics to be covered. In industry, personnel officers often make use of some ready-made framework for interviewing job applicants, such as Alec Rodger's 'Seven Point Plan', for example, or John Munro Fraser's 'Five Points'. Helpers tend to rely more on intuition, experience, and the models provided by their colleagues and agency regulations. The latter will clearly influence the kinds of questions to be asked, but most of them can be grouped under the following five headings:

1 *Description.* Physical appearance including clothes, speech, facial expression. Physical health, together with details of any illnesses or disabilities relevant to present problems. Psychological make-up; some estimate of intelligence; traits of character; attitudes and feelings.
2 *Environment.* Physical surroundings at home. Family structure. Neighbourhood.
3 *Relationships.* Extent and nature of interactions between subject and other members of family, friends, people at school, work, or in agencies and institutions.
4 *Development/experience.* A chronological account covering early development, education, training and occupation, hobbies and interests.

5 *Problems.* Description of personal difficulties, some account of their natural history, effects on subject's life. Subject's own perception of them and interviewer's evaluation.

A host of questions *can* be asked in all of these areas; the ones that *are* spring from the strategy of inquiry adopted, whether consciously or not, by the interviewer.

A common strategy employed by many investigators is to start out with a hypothesis or a number of hypotheses about the problems and their possessors which can be confirmed or rejected in the light of answers received to specific questions. These theories or suppositions represent a sort of general template gleaned from accumulated experience, against which particular cases are measured. It is a perfectly good way of going about things, so long as the templates themselves are examined from time to time, held up to the light of continuing exposure to cases, and subjected to the critical scrutiny of colleagues. It should also be borne in mind that other people have 'theoretical' models of their own.

For example, when you talk to parents about their adolescent children who are in trouble, they will sometimes refer to incidents in the child's early years when a blow to the head was suffered from falling out of the pram, or off a swing, or even a violent but accidental blow from some other source. They subscribe, in other words, to the 'hard-knock' school of deviance theory. Other parents of deviant youth subscribe to a quite different set of assumptions which revolve around themes of contamination by stronger and more odious young people out there on the street or the estate.

So besides collecting evidence to test your own theories, you should also be aware of those held by others, and be constantly open to the possibility that a new case may not fit any of the categories you habitually use.

☐ Write out an interview plan for taking a history relevant to the work you do or the people you work with. Select some topic headings, which may overlap with the five set out above, or may be quite different, and devise a comprehensive list of specific questions to ask in each area. Some of the questions should be 'closed' fact-finding ones, and others should be 'open-ended' probes and encouragements.

☐ Using the general plan you have developed for taking a history relevant to the work you do, work in a pair with someone else, and take each other's histories. Allow half an hour for the interview, and half an hour for writing up the results in a brief form. Afterwards you can discuss with your partner what it felt like to be on the receiving end. You should exchange the finished reports and comment on how accurate your partner's history of you is, and vice versa, and whether it misses out important features.

☐ Interview a colleague − a helper or would-be helper − and write a history of his/her interest in becoming a helper, the experiences which have shaped his/her motivation and the acquisition of relevant skills, concluding with some estimate of the person's strengths and weaknesses as a helper. Show the written version of your report to the person concerned and discuss its accuracy, not just at the factual level, but as a sympathetic and coherent account of a complex human situation.

Problems in the interview

No matter how careful the preparation, no matter how experienced or skilled the interviewer may be, there will always be times when things go wrong. The greater part of these problems have to do with where interviewees fall on a line representing *volubility*, that is, the willingness and ability to talk.

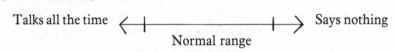

Talks all the time ⟵———————————⟶ Says nothing

Normal range

Those who talk all the time are probably a bit easier to cope with than silent individuals. They may try to monopolize the proceedings for any one of a number of reasons; they may just be gas-bags grateful for a platform and an audience of any kind; they may be lonely and suffering from verbal deprivation; they may be socially unaware people who have never grasped or mastered the principle of reciprocity in their dealings with others; they may be anxious in general, or fearful in particular about what is going to happen in the interview. It may even be a sign of aggression towards the interviewer, or the agency he/she represents. Whatever the cause, there are things to do which will slow down the over-talkative:

Ten things to do with the over-talkative
1 Ask lots of direct questions.
2 Cut them off if they stray from the point.
3 Tell them they are talking too much.
4 Offer a quicker end to the proceedings if they answer the questions.
5 Reiterate the purpose of the interview.
6 Ask a colleague to join you and keep the interview on the rails.
7 Deal with the anxiety or fear that the person is feeling.
8 Offer a general gripe session to take place when the business is concluded.
9 Pass the case to someone else.
10 Terminate the interview.

When the people you are interviewing say nothing, or next to nothing, the situation is more difficult to deal with because you have virtually no evidence on which to base your diagnosis of the problem. Are they not very intelligent? scared out of their wits? unclear about what is going on? feeling depressed? unwilling to co-operate for all sorts of private reasons? You can try to test some of these and other possibilities by asking directly about the state of mind of the person in the chair opposite, but if replies are no more forthcoming to those questions than to the rest of your efforts, then you are in deep trouble.

It may be that you remind the silent one of a disliked relative, teacher, or social worker from the past or present; or that you are simply no good at working with that kind of person, or with that person in particular. In that case, passing on responsibility to someone else is the best solution to the problem.

Michael Argyle (1978) has summarized the research on interview behaviour which elicits more responses from those being interviewed, in what can be thought of as four simple rules. These are that the interviewer should

1 Talk less.
2 Ask open-ended questions.
3 Talk about things of interest to the person being interviewed.
4 Reward the things he/she says.

Talking less may sound like a counsel of perfection when faced with a monosyllabic respondent, but the temptation is to fill the silence with nervous babble of your own invention. Otherwise the rules add up to a prescription for a more considerate and lively performance on the interviewer's part, no bad thing under any circumstances. But even when every tactic has been tried, some people's lips remain sealed. You can't win them all, and in any population of people to be interviewed there are bound to be some with whom you are personally incompatible, and some others who could not be interviewed successfully by anyone else either.

☐ Working in pairs, alternate in the roles of interviewer and talkative and/or silent subject. Conduct interviews for five minutes on neutral subjects, then discuss the experience with your partner, and with observers if you have any. Try to identify additional or alternative strategies which you could use in similar circumstances.

☐ Nominate a topic on which you would be reluctant to be interviewed — it might be your political or moral or religious views, your opinion of some person or people, your self-image, or a period in your life that was less than happy or successful — and then defy the best efforts of a partner to extract any details from you. Discuss after five minutes whether you found your colleague's tactics at all effective and if not, why not. Reverse the procedure, and discuss.

☐ Repeat the first exercise, but on each occasion appoint a third person to act as 'coach' to the interviewer. The job of the coach is to observe the performance of the interviewer, to stop the proceedings at any point to make suggestions for improvements, and to monitor the final results and discuss them with the participants.

Timing

Interviews are frequently conducted under conditions of some pressure: a deadline for a report; a waiting room full of other people waiting to be seen; other calls to be made that evening; other appointments to be kept. So one of the skills of interviewing is being able to time the proceedings so that all the necessary agenda is covered within the time available.

☐ Working in trios, agree a topic — 'leisure' would be an innocuous example — and some major headings for an interview plan. Then work independently for five minutes devising questions and making decisions about how to divide the time available during a ten-minute interview. Each person then carries out a ten-minute interview on the agreed topic, with the third person acting as adviser/producer/ coach to the interviewer, keeping an eye on the time, suggesting when to move on to another topic, or indicating other questions that ought to be asked. When all the interviews have been completed, review the exercise to see who did better or worse, and how any difficulties could be put right in future work.

Summarizing

One of the essential arts of interviewing is the ability to remember what has been said and to offer a brief summary of it to the person to whom you have been talking as a way of concluding the business of that particular meeting. In ordinary circumstances, because you have more power or prestige or influence than the interviewees, or because they are under some other kind of stress, or because they are too polite to say otherwise, your version of what has passed between you may not be challenged at the time. It may not even be challenged at a later date when it has a direct bearing upon the future life and happiness of the person concerned; that is when it has been incorporated in an official report or used as the basis of some recommendation or decision. But it may, for all that, be false, wrong, or otherwise untrue to both the spirit and the substance of the transaction from which it was allegedly drawn — namely the interview which you conducted.

You can test your ability to summarize accurately in any of a number of ways:

☐ Tape-record an interview, including the summary as you say it to the person you have just interviewed. Check its accuracy later against the tape-recording of what was actually said.

☐ Practise summarizing interviews undertaken with friends or colleagues in which you also ask them to summarize what they have said, either verbally or in writing, so that you can compare the two versions.

☐ Appoint an observer to watch some of your interviews and to comment on how faithful your subsequent summaries were to the spoken word.

☐ Ask to observe somebody else who is conducting an interview and summarizing it; make your own summary independently and compare notes afterwards.

Improving interview skills

The exercises in this chapter are intended to act in a double capacity; to help would-be helpers assess their interviewing skills; and to provide opportunities for changing or improving them. In this final section some suggestions are made about developing interview skills.

The first stage in the development of any kind of skill is to become aware of one's own performance, of its strengths and weaknesses, and of those areas where change and improvement are most needed. Self-awareness can be achieved by a variety of methods, the most obvious being simply thinking about what you do, and how you do it. This can be done in *more* or *less* structured ways but it can never altogether escape the accusation that the person involved sits as judge *and* jury in his/her own case. To introspection, therefore, must be added an element of external observation and report, a process best described by the technical term 'feedback'. This consists of information from the environment which can be used to modify the performance or behaviour of an organism. In ordinary human interaction the quality of this feedback is usually too veiled to be of much use for training purposes. It must therefore be made more immediate, more direct, and more explicit. This can be done by having third parties observe your interviewing behaviour and telling you afterwards what they thought of it. Their views and opinions can be given a little more structure by providing check-lists and rating instruments. Both self-review and that provided by external observers can be greatly facilitated through the use of video tape-recordings which allow the *same* behaviour to be viewed over and over again rather than once only.

All of these methods can be used not only to gather data about *actual* performance but also to bring about *changes* via their employment as monitoring or self-monitoring devices.

☐☐ Feedback methods

☐ Internal review
With some thought and a little practice it is possible to run through a completed interview inside one's head and to make what amounts to a mental reconstruction of it. Quite a lot of ordinary mental activity consists of day-dreaming about past events, turning them this way and that, imagining what might have been said at this point, how one might have looked, how things might have turned out differently, or more advantageously. This mechanism can be used to review and improve your interview behaviour.

After completing a practice interview, sit down somewhere quiet and run through what happened from the knock at the door to the last goodbye. If it helps, make notes of things you want to come back to, but concentrate first of all on simply remembering as much as possible of what went on. With a bit of practice most people can get quite good at this. A useful exercise is to take a quite short interview which you have recorded in sound or vision and attempt afterwards, without the aid of notes, to write down the dialogue as it occurred. Check what you have written against the recording. You can also add a commentary alongside the words or dialogue, about what else was happening, either at the non-verbal level, or inside your own head.

☐ Self-rating

Slightly more systematic impressions can be recorded about aspects of your own interviewing by using simple rating scales, on which you mark appropriate points between *positive* and *negative*.

Interview with _____ Date _____

Interviewers:	Positive				Negative
Confidence	⌊____⌊____⌊____⌊____⌋
Demeanour	⌊____⌊____⌊____⌊____⌋
Expression	⌊____⌊____⌊____⌊____⌋
Speech	⌊____⌊____⌊____⌊____⌋
Questions	⌊____⌊____⌊____⌊____⌋
Listening	⌊____⌊____⌊____⌊____⌋
Summarizing	⌊____⌊____⌊____⌊____⌋

☐ Video recording

Both reflection and self-rating can be considerably enhanced by a video-taped record of the interview in question. Never try to analyse very long extracts or complete interviews lasting for more than a few minutes; the effort is out of proportion to the returns. Concentrate on a brief period, making notes afterwards about the performance, *or* using a simple rating sheet.

The tape itself can be entirely in long-shot showing both of the parties for the duration of the encounter; or in close-up on your own face if you want to make close observation of expressions and other forms of non-verbal communication; or split-screen, if your video machinery is sufficiently sophisticated, which can show both faces in close-up at the same time. Just watching a straightforward recording can be an education in itself, revealing many facets of behaviour that are normally invisible to the *actor* but perfectly visible to everyone else.

Concentrating for the moment on non-verbal communication, some things to look for:

— differences in expression when *speaking*, and *listening*,
— direction and duration of eye-contact,
— amount of time smiling, looking serious,
— variety of expression at other times, and its appropriateness to the content of the words being exchanged, type of topic, state of the interviewee, etc.
— posture − changes and continuity, and relevance to content and tone of dialogue.
— non-verbal following, nodding, and grunting.

☐ **External review**

If difficulty is experienced with the imaginative reconstruction of an interview, or with making some assessment of your performance, either with or without the benefit of video recordings, it may be helpful to recruit someone else − a colleague, a fellow student, or a friend − and ask him/her to interview you about your performance and help you review strengths and weaknesses. The person who helps you do this need not have witnessed the encounter being considered; his/her job is simply to prompt you into going over the events as fully and systematically as possible, spotting some of the points where you think you could have done your job better.

☐ Consumers

The feedback from which helpers are most likely to shrink is that supplied by the people on the receiving end of their helping efforts. There are some obvious difficulties about this, both practical and ethical. It would not, for example, be a good idea to stop distressed applicants for aid and assistance, as they left the agency building, to ask them what they thought of the interview they had just experienced. And some of them would not be able to respond to what might appear to them to be a bureaucratic trap or official snooping on the worker they had just seen. However, it is not impossible to secure this kind of feedback, and you can start by carrying out an interview with a colleague and asking him/her to give you feedback afterwards, looking at questions like:

How well did you explain the purpose of the interview?
Did you appear to be at ease in the situation?
Were your questions intelligible?
How did the person being interviewed feel at different points?
Were there any areas left unexplored?

Following feedback from a colleague, the exercise can be repeated with a previously unknown person who is willing to discuss the interview afterwards. The final step is to secure feedback from real live interviewees, who should be chosen with care for their capacity to respond at all rather than carefully chosen in the hope that they will do so favourably. You can ask them for this feedback directly yourself; a colleague can do it for you; and you can get the individual concerned to give his/her comments verbally or by responding to a simple review format:

1 What was the purpose of the interview you have just had?
2 What was the interviewer trying to do?
3 How did you feel during the interview? Tick the statement you agree with:

Comfortable all the time   ☐
Comfortable most of the time   ☐
Comfortable some of the time   ☐
Comfortable now and then   ☐
Not at all comfortable   ☐

4 Were there any questions you did not understand? What were they?
5 Did you say most of the things you wanted to get across?
6 Were there any questions you did not want to answer?

7 How warm a person was the interviewer? Put a ring round one of these numbers.

Very warm   3   2   1   1   2   3   Not very warm

8 Do you think the interviewer understood what you were saying?

9 Is there any way that the interviewer could have done a better job? If so, how?

_____

_____

The more pieces of evidence of any sort that it is possible to assemble about interviewing behaviour, the better, and the more likely it is that you can use the feedback to make improvements in your helping skills.

The uses of feedback

The aim of all this activity is not just academic or aesthetic, it serves the practical purpose of providing guidelines for changing behaviour. If there is evidence that you come across to the people you interview in ways that you either do not intend or that appear on reflection not to be helpful, then you may wish to change what you do. So the first use of feedback is for spotting gaps, deficits and difficulties. Just a point on negative feedback: it should not be seen as wounding personal criticism, any more than a low score at darts, or a thrashing on the tennis courts represents a complete indictment of you as a person. They simply indicate the need for improvement, if you want to move up a league, or an acknowledgement on your part that your game is not good enough for the league in which you currently play. But unless you are diabolically bad at everything, it should also furnish some good news about things that are going well, about strengths and positive qualities, and those are encouraging items to set alongside the ones that point to areas where improvements are necessary.

The second major use of feedback is as a device for continuously monitoring any progress that is being made towards the targets you have set for improvements.

Practice

None of the materials in this chapter possess magical qualities for producing instantly successful interviewers; that can only be achieved by lots of practice. The exercises _can_ help to pinpoint areas which need attention, and provide opportunities for practising component skills, but they must all be combined in real-life work if they are to be effective. If you are not presently employed in a position where interviewing is part of the job, there are a great many topics on which you can do practice interviews, with relatives, friends, and acquaintances.

Some suggestions:

Life stories
— members of your family, friends, relatives, neighbours
— the story of a street or road
— the oldest person you know; about an historical event
— the working life of people of any age
— emotional histories, i.e. important relationships, and high points and low points in people's lives
— political or religious or philosophic development
— a driving history; cars they have loved (or hated)

Crises
— the death of someone close
— the end of a relationship
— a quarrel with a friend
— a sudden illness or disability
— losing a job after a long time
— failing an exam
— failing to get a job

Problems
— lack of confidence
— anxiety
— depression
— managing money
— getting satisfaction at work
— temper
— shyness
— rudeness
— dealing with children
— sorting out domestic disagreements
— being in charge of other people

You can easily add to this list some topics which will be more relevant to the particular work you do with people. The essential point, whatever the title, is to get as much practice as possible, reflecting at every stage on how well you think the encounter has gone; congratulating yourself on the positives, and noting for further work those aspects of your performance which require some improvement.

Notes and references

Despite the central importance of interviewing in a number of occupations it is not possible to recommend any really satisfactory basic introductory texts for would-be interviewers. There is of course no shortage of contributions to the literature of interviewing but it tends to be scattered about in books and journals devoted to other topics. Some of these are cautionary in tone; cf. Harold Garfinkel (1967) *Studies in Ethnomethodology* (Englewood Cliffs, N.J.: Prentice-Hall), or H. J. Eysenck (1953) *Uses and Abuses of Psychology* (Harmondsworth: Penguin).

A more positive starting point might be E. and K. de Schweinitz (1962) *Interviewing in the Social Services: An Introduction* (London: National Council of Social Service), and E. Sidney, M. Brown, and M. Argyle (1973) *Skills with People* (London: Hutchinson). The impact of the first contact with a helping agency is considered in A. S. Hall (1975) *The Point of Entry* (London: Allen and Unwin).

The whole area of non-verbal communication is best approached through the many works of Michael Argyle, e.g. M. Argyle (1978) *The Psychology of Interpersonal Behaviour*, 3rd edition (Harmondsworth: Penguin); and M. Argyle and M. Cook (1976) *Gaze and Mutual Gaze* (London: Cambridge University Press).

More specific aspects of interview behaviour are examined in innumerable studies by psychologists and others, e.g. K. Heller (1972) Interview structure and interviewer style in initial interviews, in A. W. Siegman and B. Pope (eds) *Studies in Dyadic Communication* (New York: Pergamon); and S. M. Jourard and P. E. Jaffe (1970) Influence of an interviewer's disclosure on the self-disclosure of interviewees. *Journal of Counseling Psychology* **17**: 252–59.

One of the most celebrated interview outlines in use in this country is that of Alec Rodger (1974) *Seven Point Plan* (London: NFER); see also J. M. Fraser (1971) *Introduction to Personnel Management* (London: Nelson) for a summary of his 'five points'.

4 Counselling

Sooner or later in most encounters in which one individual is understood to be helping another, the moment arrives in which the helper is expected to do something or say something that will be of value to the person being helped.

This suggestion may seem obvious enough in itself, but many primers of helping technique brim over with strategies for avoiding this awkward moment, for postponing it, or for transferring responsibility for it to someone else. One much-favoured tactic is that of diverting attention, by encouraging those involved to engage in substitute activities which appear to be 'helping' but are in fact poor imitations of it. At their worst these strategies become institutionalized; the work of a supposed 'helping' agency may be structured to ensure as far as possible that these awkward moments occur rarely if at all.

At least one of the reasons for this apparent evasiveness on the part of those charged with the responsibility of 'helping' is easy to recognize, and is quite understandable in itself. The task of aiding individuals with their personal difficulties is by no means an easy one. The activities which make up counselling – stimulating individuals to gain insights into themselves; giving support and advice to those under stress; seeing a way through some confused interpersonal predicament; or changing deeply ingrained attitudes or habits – are extremely demanding and require great subtlety and skill of those who wish to use them well. Little wonder that the intangible, complex, and sometimes enigmatic business of counselling is referred to as an 'art'.

Given how elusive the ability to counsel is, it is hardly surprising that those who possess it are often accorded the respect usually reserved for members of the medical profession. But if this attitude has as its corollary the belief that counselling is beyond the capacity of most people, then it is rather unfortunate and misleading in its effects. In this book, we would like to assert just the opposite: that almost everyone can become an effective and understanding counsellor; that the principal qualification required is a genuine interest in others and a desire to help them with their problems; and that beyond this, an individual's ability to be useful to others can be enhanced by some training exercises tailored to his or her needs.

This is not to advocate that the process of counselling can be 'de-mystified' completely. Some kinds of personal attributes obviously play a part; and the complex exchanges that take place when one individual helps another (or when any two people interact) are at present only poorly understood. Counselling cannot be fully developed on a purely 'behavioural' level. It remains true, however, that people can become better helpers by finding out about the effect they have on others, and by examining the skills they use when they interact in a 'helping' encounter. The aim of this chapter is to describe some exercises which can be used to help individuals improve their counselling skills. But first, it may be worthwhile looking briefly at the qualities of the successful counsellor as they have been identified by systematic research.

Attributes of effective helpers

A great deal of energy has been expended by psychologists and others who are interested in pinning down exactly which features of individuals contribute to their effectiveness as helpers. Unfortunately, or perhaps fortunately for present purposes, it just does not seem to be the case that good helpers are in any way personally distinct from their less effective counterparts. It has proven almost impossible to identify any particular *sort* of person who makes a significantly better helper than any other. Beyond the common finding that effective helpers tend themselves to be reasonably well-adjusted – and that individuals who are suffering major problems of their own are often handicapped in the extent to which they can help others – no other set of psychological characteristics of helpers has emerged clearly from the substantial amount of work that has been done.

When it comes to what individuals *do* when they are trying to help others, on the other hand, the picture does become a little clearer. While most of the research that has been done has focused on the process of psychotherapy as such (which perhaps tends to be a lengthier, more searching, and more demanding activity than the kind of counselling under consideration here), it can nevertheless tell us something about counselling as it is likely to be used in more common helping encounters.

The results of research are often confusing, and point in many different directions, but by and large they suggest that those who are good at helping go across to those whom they are helping as *genuine*; as exhibiting a degree of *empathy* and personal *warmth*; and as having a certain amount of *respect* for those whom they are trying to help. Related to these, effective helpers tend to have a positive regard for those they are trying to assist; and they show this to them by giving positive feedback – by reacting to them in a basically positive and accepting manner.

A number of other features of the way helpers act also seem to be important, and are related to the above aspects of the potential helper's approach. Research has suggested that effective helpers show less interest than ineffective helpers in *controlling* those whom they are helping or in controlling the helping encounter. In addition, effective helpers tend to stimulate, *to be active*, to give an impression that they know what they are doing, and to engage in instrumental (i.e. task-related) activity when engaged in the helping process. Good helpers show interest in those whom they are helping and express this in the way they behave.

Obviously, exactly how helpers behave depends on the kind of person and problem they are dealing with; on the stage the helping sequence is at; and on a host of other variables which cannot be predicted accurately on the basis of empirical research. But the above findings tend to emerge, again and again, from investigations of the helping process, together with one other result which is at the root of much of the work included in this book. The prospective helper's genuineness, warmth, and respect must be *conveyed* appropriately to the person intended to be their recipient; positive feedback must actually be felt by whoever it is given to; an active, stimulating, open approach must be *perceived* by the person on the receiving end. Good helpers, in other words, are good communicators; all the more reason why in improving individuals' counselling skills we should look at their communication skills overall. The exercises later in this chapter are concentrated on communication in all its many aspects, as the essence of the successful giving of help.

Two final points may be worth making about research on the attributes of helpers. First, odd as it may seem, there is no evidence which conclusively shows that more experienced helpers are necessarily more effective than those with little experience. Second, there is also no evidence whatever to suggest that going through any form of psychotherapy makes people into better helpers – even if they are in turn going to use that kind of therapy themselves. The best approach to 'learning to help' seems to be to examine your own values about it, and acquire some basic skills for putting yourself across to others.

What is counselling?

The word 'counselling' has a very broad frame of reference, and can mean anything from the kind of informal advice-giving that often takes place between close friends to the most complex kinds of exchanges that might occur between barristers and litigants in high court cases, or between patients and clinicians in an advanced moment of therapy. Its basic meaning revolves around the business of offering advice, something so common and so familiar that almost everyone could be said to have acted as a counsellor at some time in his or her life. But there are also a number of more formal kinds of counselling, some of them undertaken by individuals specifically appointed to an advisory role. Some of the most obvious spheres in which counselling takes place include:

— Careers counselling, sometimes called vocational guidance, carried out by some teachers and by the Youth Employment Service and related agencies, is aimed especially at helping individuals to find and make decisions about jobs.

— Social work, which involves counselling on a very wide range of problems, from finance or accommodation difficulties to family, legal, or personal issues, or problems connected with having broken the law.
— Pastoral counselling in schools and colleges, which is designed to help individuals with problems not only which affect their learning, but are also having an impact on broader aspects of their self-development.
— Marriage guidance counselling, undertaken by probation officers or by specially trained workers from the Marriage Guidance Council is concerned with advice-giving and conflict resolution on marital and other family problems.
— Voluntary and statutory advice centres have grown up in recent years to supplement the work of social services departments; their principal aim is to give help with practical problems to do with money, rights, or accommodation, or on specific topics such as drugs.

Obviously a great many other categories of individuals, such as doctors, solicitors, or estate agents for example, give people advice of particular kinds, but they are not for the most part asked for help with very personal problems, nor is this seen by most people as a central aspect of their jobs.

Within its loosely defined 'advice-giving' function, counselling in fact is used to fulfil a large number of specific aims:

1 *Information giving.* In this respect counselling is a bit like 'one-to-one teaching'. Some problems can be solved simply by the provision of facts and many of the problems with which various counsellors deal derive from a lack of information to some extent.
2 *Promoting insight.* In other instances, counselling may be best used to help individuals find out more about themselves; to assist the process of self-discovery. With many personal and emotional difficulties, a clearer self-knowledge is the key to their solution.
3 *Giving support.* Some personal problems are so intractable and some individuals are beset with so many problems, or are so helpless in themselves, that counselling has to consist almost entirely of lending them emotional support, warmth, and the feeling that they are understood.
4 *Conflict resolution.* In certain kinds of counselling the aim of the helping process may be to diminish the animosity between two or more individuals, or help them in spite of their feelings to come to terms with each other in other areas of common interest.
5 *Problem solving.* Although most kinds of counselling can be viewed as 'problem solving' in some respect, there are also many counselling episodes in which the overall aim is to help individuals to systematically analyse difficulties, find solutions to them, and put these into effect.
6 *Decision making.* One of the most obvious aims served by counselling is that of helping people to make decisions which they are finding difficult to reach, either because of some situation's inherent complexity or because the individual's ability to take decisions

has temporarily broken down. The counsellor may help the person to weigh up *pros* and *cons*; may offer suggestions for his or her perusal; or may broaden the perspective within which a particular problem is approached.

Counselling consists, then, of several different elements or strands, the exact amounts of which vary from one helping encounter to another, and the overall balance in each case often being very difficult to assess.

Dimensions of counselling

Not only does the nature of counselling vary according to the setting in which it is practised, and according to the exact aims which it is designed to serve; it also depends on a number of other factors which can be roughly characterized as 'approach'. There are innumerable ways to go about counselling, but it is possible to describe them in terms of a number of dimensions along which they vary. These dimensions themselves may be construed in a number of ways but some of the more important ones are:

1 THE AMOUNT OF EMPHASIS PLACED ON THE NATURE OF THE 'COUNSELLING RELATIONSHIP'

To some counsellors, the kind of relationship they build up with those whom they are trying to help is seen as the principal theme of the work they will do and the principal vehicle for change. By getting to know the person, and sharing his or her picture of the world, as it were, the counsellor can give support and be more effective in finding solutions to problems. Often the building up of a 'therapeutic relationship' becomes an end in itself. While no approach to counselling would ever dismiss the importance of this relationship entirely, there are other views of counselling which see relationship building or enhancing as incidental, and which place greater accent on what the counsellor will say and do regardless of the distance between helper and helped.

2 'DIRECTIVE' VERSUS 'NON-DIRECTIVE' COUNSELLING

Another way in which counsellors differ is in the extent to which they attempt to directly influence the person they are attempting to help — by making suggestions, initiating action, proposing solutions, and so on. This is 'directive' counselling and carried to the extreme is a potentially destructive approach if it ignores individuals' sensitivities or makes them more defensive by goading them into actions which they are incapable of taking. At the other end of the continuum is the completely non-directive counsellor, who concentrates on helping individuals to clarify what they are thinking, who rarely makes suggestions, and who acts as if individuals already possess the solutions to their problems and all they have to do is to discover them. Obviously this can be unproductive for quite different reasons. Some kind of balance between these two opposites seems advisable, and it is useful for prospective helpers to become aware of the degree to which they are inclined to be 'directive' or not.

3 DEGREE OF STRUCTURE

Approaches to counselling also vary in the extent to which they insist that the counselling process should follow a prearranged pattern, or should be wholly flexible and dependent on the person being helped. In other words, whereas some counsellors adopt particular psychological theories as a basis for their work, and then obviously interpret what they see and follow a prescribed sequence of activities in the light of them, others take a much more 'open' stance and are prepared to try to comprehend individuals in their own terms. Clearly it is almost impossible to avoid some prejudices and assumptions about people when we engage in counselling of any kind: the difference here is in terms of the level of development of our ideas about others − and the extent to which they are 'structured' or 'formalized' along the lines of a particular theory or 'school'.

4 RELIANCE ON PARTICULAR TECHNIQUES

Associated with the foregoing is another 'dimension' of counselling: the degree to which the counsellor undertakes his or her work through the medium of special methods (which will almost always be derived from whichever theoretical orientation he or she espouses). Some counsellors always use certain ways of working and never use others. A few use a wide range of helping methods irrespective of their 'theoretical' source. Some theories of how individuals think, act, and change are very far removed from everyday common sense; others are rooted very closely in daily life and can be immediately recognized by someone in need of help. Would-be helpers need to make up their minds about the extent to which they want to entertain ways of working with others which are at first sight unfamiliar and apparently at odds with their proclaimed aims.

Phases of counselling

It is difficult to take such a fluid, complex process as counselling and divide it up into neat, clearly defined stages; every helping encounter is likely to be different and the perceptions of the individuals involved in it may be quite at variance with one another. However for training purposes it can be useful to identify a number of 'phases' of counselling. Although these will often overlap with one another (particularly in the central stages), the exercise can furnish a means of isolating separate counselling skills. The following list sets out one possible analysis of counselling.

1 *Establishing contact* – opening the relationship; helping people to relax; exchanging first impressions.

2 *Exploration and assessment* – the phase in which individuals are encouraged to talk about their problems; the counsellor asks questions, collects information, seeks views, and possibly helps the individual to arrive at a clearer definition of his/her problem.

3 *Building a relationship* – unless the problems are absolutely simple and easily solved, the counsellor will want to get to know the person better and develop a better understanding of his or her views. This may entail disclosing more about him- or herself. This activity and the previous one are in many helping encounters simultaneous.

4 *Influencing* – a further development of helping occurs where the counsellor is asked to give advice to the person with the problem, which might involve encouraging change, controlling the direction which counselling takes, joint problem solving, information giving, making suggestions, or possibly confrontation.

5 *Monitoring and sustaining change* – if individuals are pursuing complex or long-term goals, or are going through further difficulties or personal changes, the counsellor might then be required to give support, evaluate progress, comment on successes and failures, or otherwise help individuals consolidate any gains they have made.

6 *Terminating or withdrawing support* – if or when individuals achieve their desired goals, the counsellor has done his or her job and can estimate the overall value to the individual of what has transpired, which will signal either the end of the 'counselling partnership' or the need to return to an earlier stage to tackle problems in a novel way.

The skills training approach

As in the other chapters of this book, the approach to counselling that is set out here is concerned primarily with the kinds of *skill* that individuals need to develop if they are to become confident and competent helpers. This approach does not deny the importance of the relationship between helper and helped, but focuses most attention on how skills for building up this relationship can be acquired and improved. Nor does this approach suggest that individuals need to transform themselves in order to become useful to others; we can all 'act natural', or be ourselves the more thoroughly if we examine our behaviour towards others and alter it slightly if we think it is giving the *wrong* impression. To propose that helpers can improve the way they deal with others while at the same time remaining themselves is quite different from suggesting that they put a 'professional' distance between themselves and the people they are trying to help.

This chapter is divided into two main sections:

1 *Self-assessment of counselling skills.* The best starting-point for the development of skills is an examination by individuals of those areas in which they have varying levels of skill in dealing with others. This will enable them to set their own learning goals in relation to the components of 'counselling skill'.

2 *Training exercises.* The bulk of the chapter contains a variety of exercises for acquiring or improving particular counselling skills; these are organized under two headings:

(a) *Attending skills.* The provision of worthwhile help depends absolutely on the helper's ability to understand the problem as it is seen by the person experiencing it; the exercises in this section are designed to help individuals improve their skills in this respect.

(b) *Influencing skills.* Most helping encounters then move on to the giving of advice, support, or suggestions as to how a problem might be solved. At this stage the helper is, like it or not, involved in influencing the person's life to some degree. This section described training exercises which can be used to develop abilities of this kind.

It is impossible, of course, to prescribe exactly how any given individual or issue ought to be dealt with in a counselling session, and no attempt is made in any of these exercises to provide *solutions* to the kinds of problems with which counsellors are asked to help. Towards the end of the chapter, however, a number of exercises are included which may help individuals develop a flexible approach to counselling and anticipate some of the difficulties that might arise during counselling to frustrate the 'helping process'.

There are, it need hardly be said, many more aspects of counselling than can possibly be included in a book of this size and scope. Those who would like to extend particular exercises in new directions, or who believe that any particular skill or kind of event has been neglected in what follows, are encouraged to devise other exercises for themselves.

Some of the exercises described here can be undertaken by individuals working alone and a few call for large groups. The majority, however, are designed for use in small groups (say between three and ten members), in which 'trainees' or students can participate in assessing themselves and each other, giving each other feedback, keeping records, and so on – as was the case with interviewing. This is what is sometimes known as 'micro-training' and its effectiveness (and enjoyability) can be considerably enhanced by having a video tape machine available. Then, when some group members practise a particular skill in a role-play, others can act as 'observers', and others can be responsible for recording the sequence and playing it back on a television monitor. The teacher, tutor, or supervisor – if there is one – might organize the session overall, and lead a discussion at various junctures to bring out salient points. In the absence of such a person, training exercises of this kind can be self-organized by group members. Whatever the case, users of these exercises will have to make their own decisions as to exactly how each of them should be carried out.

Self-assessment

The first batch of exercises to be considered here is concerned with the process of *self-assessment* in counselling. An awareness of yourself, of your impact on others, and of your strengths and weaknesses in dealing with them, is an essential prerequisite of any training

A 'micro-training' session: role-play with observers and video recording

designed to improve helping skills. The basic mechanism of the exercises to be described here is that of trying out various skills in a small group context, and of inviting and obtaining feedback from peers as to the appropriateness of what you have said or done. Most exercises focus, therefore, on specific pieces of behaviour, and on the attitudes associated with them, as they might manifest themselves at different points in a standard 'helping' encounter.

The exercises invite participants to use role-play to analyse, assess, and practise a variety of interpersonal skills that are indispensable tools in effective counselling. Special emphasis is placed on the observation and recording of 'counsellor behaviour' in role-plays, followed by feedback to the would-be 'counsellor' of the ratings, comments, and views of others.

USING ROLE-PLAY TO LOOK AT COUNSELLING

As in the preceding chapter, one of the basic methods that will be used here to help individuals appraise and alter their own social behaviour will be that of *role-play*. The fundamental idea is still the same: that of recreating a real-life social encounter in miniature, and in an artificial way, for the purpose of analysing what is going on, assessing the performance of various participants, and giving individuals feedback with which they

A 'micro-training' session: subsequent playback and discussion

can improve their social skills. Role-playing is, perhaps unfortunately, very difficult to do alone: it can be done, but the results tend to be fairly predictable! It might be as well if you are engaged in training to plunge straight in and try some role-plays of simple two-person counselling situations.

□□ Form a pair with someone else and try to enact some familiar 'helping' encounter in which one of you asks the other for some kind of advice. This may be about a money problem, a decision at work, something to do with a personal relationship, or may be to help someone make up his or her mind on a thorny issue arising from conflicting beliefs or opinions. Act this scene through for four or five minutes and then comment on the experience and on what you said to each other.

To limber things up further, you can develop this by doing a 'role-reversal' exercise. All this means is that the positions of 'helper' and 'person with the problem' are swapped round. This should help you to prepare yourself further for the future use of role-play; to become used to the idea of role-play, and adept in applying it, you have to be able to take on different roles at different points and to comply with new definitions of who you are.

Many kinds of fairly uncomplicated two-person exchanges can be role-played in this fashion. People can play them first one way and then with roles reversed. Situations that lend themselves to this sort of exercise are not hard to find. For example:

— A parent asks a teacher about the progress of a child at school.
— An individual asks a social worker about sources of help with a handicapped child.
— An advice centre worker is asked for help concerning someone's debt problems.
— An offender asks his/her probation officer for advice concerning accommodation difficulties.

Participants in an exercise of this kind will have to embellish these brief outlines with detail — made up on the spur of the moment — to make the role-plays as lifelike as possible. For the purpose of this exercise this kind of veracity is not all that important; the real aim of the exercise is just to help trainees become accustomed to the idea of role-play as such. If you have trouble inventing situations for role-plays, the box below contains some other suggestions that you could use.

The general format of two-person role-play can be used to assess and train behaviour in many counselling situations. However, actors in role-plays are often too involved in what they are doing to be able to comment in much depth on how well they have performed. They should therefore be given feedback from some other source. This can be supplied either by observers, or by a video recording of role-plays for future playback.

For example, having established the essential technique of role-play itself, you might then carry out further role-plays in which observers are installed. Let us take one situation from the list below and see how it can be set up in this way. Individuals form small groups of three; one plays the part of a worker at the Samaritans, another rings up with a problem of some kind (feeling lonely or depressed; upset over a relationship that has just broken up; panic-stricken about exams), and a third watches the exchange and comments afterwards on what was going on. In a large group, the 'observers' can then be invited to report back to the group as a whole. In addition, the members of each trio can switch round roles, so that each has a chance to be worker, person in need of help, and observer in turn. The central mechanism of skills training has now been established amongst the members of your group. The exercise can be repeated with any of the other situations listed opposite; but a still more profitable step would be to ask group members to make up incidents of their own — based on things which had happened to them, or which were on their minds — and role-play some of these. Other exercises utilizing observers will be described in more detail below.

☐☐ **Some simple counselling situations**

1 A counsellor has to give careers advice to someone about to leave school.
2 One individual has to make a list of suggestions to the other about possible leisure pursuits in the local area.
3 Someone asks advice on how to go about claiming supplementary benefits.
4 An advice centre worker is asked by someone about the procedure for making complaints about the police.
5 A parent asks advice of a social worker about dealing with an aggressive child.
6 One person asks another for help with a drink problem or a money problem.
7 A lonely, isolated person rings the Samaritans 'for someone to talk to'.
8 Someone about to leave prison asks another for help with accommodation.
9 Someone in a helping agency feels overworked and asks his/her boss for advice.
10 Two people with a problematic marriage go to Marriage Guidance for help.
11 A young offender on supervision is being asked by a probation officer/ social worker why he/she didn't come to two previous appointments.
12 A middle-aged man who has just been made redundant goes to the Occupational Guidance Unit for help.
13 A school-leaver or young person on the dole asks someone for advice about going from a rural area to look for work in London.
14 A distraught mother of three asks for financial help because her benefit payments have been suspended without explanation.
15 An old person who is suffering from insomnia asks for help from a health visitor.

ANALYSING COUNSELLING SKILLS

Before embarking on a training programme in counselling, it may be worthwhile pausing to think about the various elements that go together to make up the ability to counsel. You can try this in several ways.

☐ Simply work by yourself and think about the process of counselling either (a) as you have been engaged in it in your own work, or (b) in as broad-based a manner as possible, taking all the contexts of counselling you can think of into account. Make a list of all the different things a good counsellor needs to be able to do; focusing particularly on what actually goes on in a counselling session, and the specific skills that are involved.

☐ Alternatively, undertake a similar exercise to the previous one in a group of two or three people. Assume that you are assembling and piloting a 'Counsellor Skills Checklist' and that you are trying to generate items for it. Break down counselling into as many identifiable skills as possible.

☐ Set up a brief role-play in which someone poses as a counsellor and another person poses as an individual needing help. The help could be anything – careers advice; about a debt of some kind; suggestions as to how to cope with a difficult child. Observe the person who is acting as 'helper' and make a list of as many different things as possible that the person seems to be doing. If a number of observers do this simultaneously they can then compare to see how many common items they have arrived at; and this can be the basis of a counsellor skills check-list as in the foregoing exercise.

SELF-RATINGS OF COUNSELLING SKILLS

Such a complex kind of behaviour as counselling can obviously be analysed in very many different ways, but to improve counselling skills we have to begin somewhere and in this exercise you are asked to rate yourself according to how good you think you are at some of the components of the counsellor's repertoire of skills.

The self-rating sheet opposite asks you to say how good you think you are at each of twenty-five different constituents of counselling. Clearly, your own perceptions of this and other people's may be at variance with one another; but a valuable first step in training is self-assessment and you are asked to concentrate here on giving *your* ratings of your own competence.

When you have completed the exercise it may be useful to make a list of the items you think you're best at (scores of 5, or of 4 and 5 if there are very few 5s); and another list of the things you think you're worst at (scores of 1 or of 1 and 2). These lists can then form a starting-point for some of the training later in the chapter.

You may also find it valuable to compare your ratings with those of other people; especially if you are working alongside someone on whose skills you could comment or who might comment on yours. You could compare each other's self-ratings and see whether you agree or disagree with the scores you have given yourselves.

□□ **Counselling skills**

The list of skills shown here is designed to help you identify those parts of the counselling process about which you feel confident and competent, together with those parts in which you would like to improve your ability. Rate each skill on a 5-point scale, as follows:

1 means I am *never* good at that skill
2 means I am *seldom* good at that skill
3 means I am *sometimes* good at that skill
4 means I am *usually* good at that skill
5 means I am *always* good at that skill

□□ **Counselling skills — self-ratings**

1 Introducing yourself	1	2	3	4	5
2 Listening — taking in what people say	1	2	3	4	5
3 Listening — showing interest in people	1	2	3	4	5
4 Communicating feelings	1	2	3	4	5
5 Responding to anger	1	2	3	4	5
6 Responding to praise	1	2	3	4	5
7 Responding to expressions of anxiety	1	2	3	4	5
8 Responding to flippancy	1	2	3	4	5
9 Coping with apathy and expressions of disinterest	1	2	3	4	5
10 Coping with silence	1	2	3	4	5
11 Appreciating other people's feelings	1	2	3	4	5
12 Giving information	1	2	3	4	5
13 Giving advice on emotional problems	1	2	3	4	5
14 Reflecting	1	2	3	4	5
15 Asking open-ended questions	1	2	3	4	5
16 Waiting for replies	1	2	3	4	5
17 Changing the direction of conversations	1	2	3	4	5
18 Expressing support	1	2	3	4	5
19 Disclosing things about yourself if necessary	1	2	3	4	5
20 Making a conversation more serious	1	2	3	4	5
21 Making a conversation less serious	1	2	3	4	5
22 Summarizing what people have said	1	2	3	4	5
23 Holding someone's interest and attention	1	2	3	4	5
24 Interpreting people's motives	1	2	3	4	5
25 Ending sessions in a positive way	1	2	3	4	5

SELF-OBSERVATION AND THE USE OF OBSERVERS

In the process of analysing counsellor skills, individuals were asked to set up an artificial 'counselling session' and to observe the behaviour of someone role-playing a counsellor in action. This kind of observational exercise is an invaluable one for skills training and will be used as the basis of, or as an adjunct to, many of the training methods to be suggested later in the chapter.

Interacting with others involves sending them messages of many kinds simultaneously – by means of the voice, face, gestures, body posture, use of the eyes, and occupation of the space between you and them. Effective communication uses all of these different kinds of signal at once; and although in ordinary everyday intercourse we assimilate all of these in conjunction, in some instances we may feel awkward because someone seems to be acting in an inappropriate way and we can't quite identify why. Communication is at its clearest when all the different kinds of signals we can 'transmit' flow in concert; when this is not the case, our meaning is likely to be misunderstood.

The accompanying observer ratings sheet is intended to enable observers to analyse the different constituents of social behaviour while it is in progress. Observers watch others taking part in a role-play – or look at their own performance as recorded on video – and rate what they see in terms of the various items marked out on the sheet. The results should then be passed on to the person whom they were observing.

One way of using a sheet like this is to make, in company with other group members, brief video recordings of role-plays in which you take part; or alternatively, to conduct 'live' role-plays in which two people act as helper and helpee and others observe what is going on. Some possible suggestions for brief role-plays of this kind were given above (p. 63).

When using a sheet like this, it is impossible to rate more than one person at a time; so if you're running a role-play which involves several different people, you'll need to divide the observers into pairs or trios each assigned to observe one participant in the action (for example as shown in the illustration below).

Judgements of what is 'appropriate' as regards the various items on the sheet will almost certainly vary from one person to another. This is interesting in itself and you should compare ideas on this, as well as actual ratings, to look for similarities and differences.

As will be suggested below (repeatedly), ratings like these should not be seen as scores which indicate something immutable about an individual. They are the building blocks of skills training; someone who, for example, uses gestures or expressions in an inappropriate way may wish to learn how to use them more skilfully. Group members may suggest more appropriate gestures, expressions, etc. to the person in question who should then try to deploy these in a re-run of the role-play. 'Feedback' from observers then becomes an instrument by which the individual can gauge his or her progress in improving counselling skills.

An exercise like this could be applied to each of the specific skills listed on the self-ratings

☐☐ **Observer ratings**

Your task as an observer is to watch the person engaged as counsellor in the role-play, or to observe your own performance on video, and rate the behaviour you see on the scales below. You are particularly interested in the appropriateness of the counsellor's use of different 'channels' of communication.

The rating scale should be used as follows:

1 – used appropriately throughout
2 – used appropriately most of the time
3 – sometimes appropriate, but equally often not
4 – fairly erratic and inappropriate
5 – completely erratic and inappropriate

Eye contact, focus of gaze	1	2	3	4	5
Personal spacing and distance	1	2	3	4	5
Gestures (hand and head)	1	2	3	4	5
Body posture	1	2	3	4	5
Facial expressions	1	2	3	4	5
Tone of voice	1	2	3	4	5
Timing of speech	1	2	3	4	5
General co-ordination of all the above	1	2	3	4	5

Now use the other rating scales below to make some more general comments about the counsellor's performance:

1 How clear was the voice of the person playing the counsellor?
  Very clear ⌞_____⌟ Not at all clear

2 How confident did the counsellor seem to be?
  Very confident ⌞_____⌟ Not at all confident

3 How interested did he/she seem in the person's problem?
  Very interested ⌞_____⌟ Not at all interested

sheet used previously. Obviously this would take a long time and might become very tedious if everyone in a group were to do the same. It may be best to concentrate, therefore, on the skills that most need attention.

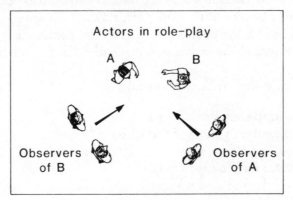

EXPLORING COUNSELLING IN PEER INTERVIEWS

If you are working with other people in counsellor training, it would be very unwise not to take as much advantage as possible of the opportunities that group learning presents. Comparing your views with those of others; pooling ideas; working jointly on a project; or just observing each other's reactions to training, can all add considerably to both the enjoyment and the effectiveness of any learning experience.

Peer interviews are guided conversations between two or more individuals aimed primarily at enabling them to examine each other's opinions on a given topic. For counselling, these could be centred on a wide spectrum of issues, as for example:

— Why I am interested in counselling.
— A difficult problem I had to deal with.
— The most awkward person I've ever met.
— Skills I would like to improve.
— Problems I enjoy dealing with.
— Problems I like to avoid.
— My ideal caseload.
— Two people I'd like to bring together.
— A particular moment I felt afraid/pleased/angry/embarrassed about.

Discussion on topics like these and many others can be used as a vehicle for helping individuals engaged in training (a) to get to know one another better; (b) to find out about the range of views on particular issues; (c) to compare personal feelings and attitudes with those of others; (d) to practise the skills of asking questions, listening, and responding; and (e) to explore the kinds of problems that may arise in counselling, and give some preliminary thought to how they might deal with them.

Following a peer interview session in which individuals have spoken to perhaps two or three others in their group, it will be useful to obtain feedback from them about the exercise, whom they spoke to, and what they might have learnt.

'Attending' skills

Broadly speaking, the business of counselling involves the worker in two distinct kinds of activities − though they clearly interplay with each other in a subtle and complex way during the process of counselling itself. The first is *attending*. There is an obvious and fundamental need, if you are trying to give someone help, to listen to what he or she is saying, to try to understand him or her as an individual, to appreciate his or her point of view, and to gather information that will be necessary for any decisions that might be made or advice that might be given later on. Afterwards, when the helper has become better acquainted with the person − has assembled some facts about his or her problems, has established some basis for conjoint action, and has given some thought as to the best way to proceed − the second kind of activity comes into play: that of *influencing*. It is at this point that the helper seeks to have some impact on an individual's life, not in any 'interfering' manner, but on the principle of giving assistance as and when it may be required.

Although the analysis of the counselling process outlined earlier suggested that counselling could be viewed in terms of a number of different phases, the activities of attending and influencing are central regardless of the particular phase counselling may have reached. One way to look at the progress of counselling is in terms of the relative balance of the two activities which has been struck at a given moment. This can even be represented in the form of a diagram like the one shown here. Earlier on in the counselling relationship, the helper must concentrate as much as possible on the person requesting help, and must understand as much as possible of what that person says before moving on to the next stage. But even at this point, *some* kinds of 'influence' are being exerted − in the form of the specific questions that are asked, the responses given to them, the impression given by the helper to the person being helped, and the implication this may have for the way they will subsequently behave towards each other. Later, the helper's influencing skills come to the fore, when the helper must somehow 'deliver the goods' and prove useful to the person on

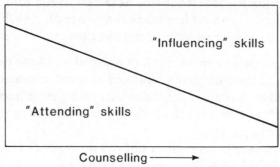

the receiving end. But here also the helper still has to be responsive to what the person in need of help says; must be aware of his or her reactions, open to comments, and must continue gathering information, making assessments, and furthering his or her understanding of the individual's plight. Thus, while the early phases of counselling are dominated by attending on the part of the helper, later phases are dominated by influencing; but in neither case does one kind of activity totally exclude the other.

The exercises in this section are concerned with the skills that are part and parcel of successful 'attending' to others; listening to what they have to say; negotiating a first encounter with them; asking them questions in an appropriate way; and reading their emotional states from facial expressions and other non-verbal 'cues'.

'OPENERS'

When you meet someone for the first time there are a number of fixed gambits which are universally acceptable as openers for conversations. Socially skilled people are able to modify these subtly to suit the demands of a particular person or a particular situation. But beginning to help people is often a situation in which special forces are at work. Individuals' initial reactions to the helper may count for more than they do under ordinary circumstances. For this reason it can be valuable to anticipate and to practise dealing with the early moments of meetings with different sorts of people.

☐☐ This exercise asks you to 'model', or perform in front of your peers, the actions you would make and the words you would use when first greeting a number of people who have come to you for help. The people you have to greet can be specified in advance and might include, for example

— A very shy fourteen-year-old girl.
— An adult male offender in his mid-thirties whom you know has committed very serious offences.
— A slightly pompous middle-aged, upper-middle class man or woman.
— A lonely, isolated old lady.
— An offender in his/her late teens who has come to you with a colleague's forewarning that nobody so far has managed to handle him/her.
— A middle-aged, red-faced man in ragged clothing who smells of drink.

To do this exercise properly you have to imagine that you have read or heard something of most of the above persons beforehand — a not unrealistic prescription in most helping agencies. If certain individuals in your group find it difficult to portray what they would do in some of these situations, others should be invited to role-play some of the above parts.

The main question here is whether or not you do react differently when you are approached by different sorts of people; and whether you would like to change the way you react (either to make it more uniform or more diverse). Observers or video feedback could be used to help you build up a clearer picture of yourself in this respect.

LISTENING SKILLS

Listening is a crucial ingredient of all helping. If we do not pay attention to others, we cannot possibly understand them or furnish them with the help they need. Yet in many everyday circumstances it often becomes obvious that people are not listening to each other; an embarrassing moment, but all the more so if the listener is alleged to be there to help the person who is talking.

There are two different aspects of good listening skill. The first is the mental, or cognitive ability to register, absorb, and relay back a message which someone is giving. The second is a social skill – the ability to convey to a speaker that you are paying attention to what he or she is saying (assuming that you are), and even to react in such a way that you encourage the speaker to talk to you in as frank and relaxed a way as possible, or at least in a way that will prove useful to him or her. The exercises below are addressed to each of these aspects of listening ability.

☐☐ Absorbing and summarizing

Listening can be practised in many ways. Perhaps the simplest is to read people a short passage from a newspaper, or to tell people a story, or describe an incident, and ask them to repeat back as much as they can remember. Obviously a number of factors will be at work here – their memory power, for example, or the content of the story and how well it is read. But individuals can, with practice, absorb progressively greater amounts of information and can learn to concentrate more keenly on what someone is saying. Passages of more than about 150–200 words will probably be the longest it is practicable to use for this purpose.

Part of the skill of taking in larger amounts of information than this lies in condensing material into its most important components. This can be practised by asking people to listen to much longer passages – lasting say three or four minutes – and to relay back what they think are the major points being made or the key elements of the message. If the initial passage consists of a series of paragraphs, each with a one-sentence summary, the individual's success in managing to précis the essential content of the message can then be assessed.

☐ Verbal prompts

If one individual has been listening to another attentively, and the speaker unexpectedly stops, another aspect of listening skill will be called into play: the ability of the listener to encourage the speaker to 'go on'. Ask pairs of individuals to practise this skill. One member of each pair prepares a short talk to give to the other.

But unknown to the listener, the speaker deliberately plans to stop short at some point, to go off the point, or to simply let his/her voice trail off. The object of the exercise is then to assess how the listener steers the speaker back on to the subject, induces him/her to finish the story, etc. Observers then comment on the success of the tactics used.

☐ **Missing link**

A similar deception can be used to appraise listeners' attentiveness by asking individuals to prepare short talks or stories in which there is a vital element missing. Using peer interviews or role-plays with observers, small groups then assess whether or not listeners spotted the missing item, and how they directed attention to it, or asked for it to be filled in.

☐ **Following responses**

Most people who are genuinely listening to what someone else is saying show that they are by a series of involuntary acts. They may nod their heads, make gestures, smile or contort their faces to mirror the feelings being expressed, mutter monosyllables such as 'yes', 'oh', or 'mmm', and generally signal their interest by standing or sitting in a particular way. Using a similar format to that in the preceding exercises, these 'following responses' can be monitored by observers (using the rating sheet on p. 67), or the interview can be recorded on video for the benefit of the trainee listeners themselves. Playback – or feedback – should focus on the basic methods by which people show interest or disinterest, and on whether or not particular individuals would like to improve their 'following' skills.

Simple nods and 'umms' will not in themselves be sufficient, however, to convince people that you are interested in what they are saying over an extended conversation. Following responses have to be suited to what a speaker is saying; it is often when someone makes an inappropriate comment on what we have just said that we realize they haven't been listening. A good counsellor will show that he or she is listening to someone by making suitable comments, gestures, or expressions that dovetail neatly with a speaker's discourse. These more complex kinds of following responses may consist of (a) repetitions or paraphrases of something a speaker has just said; (b) linking statements – reactions to what the speaker has just said which also loosely anticipate what he or she might say next; (c) questions designed to elicit more information or to keep someone talking; or (d) summaries of or references to some of the things the speaker has said previously. Here are some examples of these kinds of following responses:

1 *Repetition/paraphrase*
   A: Well the first time she came back late I wasn't all that worried; the second time I began to wonder what was going on; another couple of times it's happened since then and each time I get more and more worried that she's been seeing someone else.

B (counsellor): So every time it's happened it's made you feel worse and more suspicious of her.

A: Yes and I just don't know what to do or say, I mean if nothing was happening I'd look pretty stupid, or jealous. . . .

2 *Use of linking statements*

A: . . . and then he told me that he couldn't even pay me back for last week because he'd already spent this week's pocket money –

B: I'll bet that made you feel mad.

A: You're not kidding it did! I told him that was definitely the last time he could count on me for a loan, or anything else for that matter. . . .

3 *Questions*

A: Well it's my dad who's the worst, I can't do anything right for him these days, he just won't believe there aren't any jobs in the area.

B: What exactly does he say to you then?

A: Well he tells me it's my fault I'm unemployed, if I looked harder or if I'd worked harder at school I. . . .

4 *Summaries*

A: On Friday nights we usually go into the centre of town for a couple of drinks, and sometimes we go to a club afterwards. . . .

(B nods.)

A: . . . only last Friday we just happened to run into some old mates of Joe's, and they were suggesting we go with them to this party – actually quite a long way away. . . .

B: Yes.

A: . . . I wasn't all that keen and looking back on it I wish I'd said no but Joe was keen to go. . . .

B: Mmm.

A: . . . it was only after we left the pub and I realized they were driving round in a car they'd nicked I knew there was going to be trouble –

B: Hang on, you were with Joe, and they were Joe's friends, and you didn't know the car was stolen, and neither did he? Is that right?

A: Yeah, it wasn't till we were driving along that Joe's mate said 'What do you think of the machine then Joe?' that we discovered. . . .

In the last example, although the worker is responding only minimally to the story as it gradually unfolds, he or she draws it together from time to time, and demonstrates that he or she is listening by summarizing a few of the speaker's prior statements.

Again, an individual's skill in using these methods of following can be observed by others or by him- or herself if a counselling sequence is recorded on video. If someone seems to be missing opportunities to use responses of this kind, and is thereby giving an impression of disinterest, other observers might comment on possible responses that could have been made to convey more interest and to keep the whole interaction flowing more productively.

Two final points should be borne in mind about listening and the use of following responses. First, there is no point in making a response of this kind to something someone says to you which doesn't make sense, which isn't clear, or which you don't understand: if this happens you must politely stop the speaker and ask him or her to repeat what he or she has said. This in itself will be enough to indicate that you have been paying attention and attach enough importance to what has been said to want to get it clear. Second, there is also no point in blindly and mechanically responding to a speaker if he or she is wandering aimlessly over irrelevancies far removed from the point. Under these circumstances, counsellors must find a way of steering the conversation back to its proper path. Following responses are not devices for just keeping people talking or pretending that you're listening when you're not.

It is impossible to prescribe accurately the kinds of responses individuals ought to make when they are listening to and trying to show interest in others. Some apparently completely inattentive people turn out, on questioning, to have been listening very carefully to everything another has said. Still, it is possible to identify some general features of attentive and inattentive behaviour. The photographs illustrate some moments of attention and inattention during one-to-one counselling sessions.

'Good listening' means looking a lot at the person who is speaking, adopting an attentive posture, and showing interest via facial expressions.

'Bad listening' − or not listening at all − can easily be detected in terms of the listener's direction of gaze, body movements, and inattentive expressions.

☐ You can assess the importance of 'appearing to listen' by observing conversations in which you are involved. When you are speaking to someone, you can estimate the amount of attention he/she is paying you, and by subtle questioning establish whether or not this is correlated with genuine listening. Alternatively, when you are listening to someone else, see if you can affect the amount he/she talks by deliberately switching your listening responses 'on' and 'off'.

ASKING QUESTIONS

In interviewing, we looked at the groundwork that has to be laid, and the information that has to be gathered, before helpers can proceed to actually give advice, support, or whatever else may be needed to those who have asked for their assistance. During a counselling session, other questions may have to be asked, in other ways, for a variety of purposes linked to the decision-making, insight-giving, or problem-solving function of the activity that is taking place. A number of different aspects of the use of questions can be brought out with the exercises below.

☐ **Reflective or paraphrase questions**
It occasionally happens, when individuals are describing something which is emotionally loaded for them, or which they find difficult to talk about for any other reason, that they may stop, may become muddled, or may make a series of unsuccessful attempts to express their feelings or describe something that has happened to them. In these circumstances it may be necessary to ask questions to encourage them to continue, which at one and the same time show that they are being understood and appreciated. This delicate skill can be examined briefly in role-plays designed especially for the purpose, or can be extracted from longer video recordings of whole counselling interviews.

Using role-play, ask some of your friends to play the parts of people requiring help who for various reasons wander or stop in the middle of their conversation with a 'counsellor'. The counsellor's task is then to invite them to carry on by the appropriate use of 'reflective' or 'paraphrase' questions, that is, questions which reword what the individual has said, but present it to him/her as a question which will leave things open for him/her to continue.

☐ **Asking for clarification**
In other cases questions have to be asked merely because the counsellor feels unclear as to what the 'client' is saying. Would-be counsellors are presented with a series of muddled or disconnected statements; or with a number of incomplete facts related to a problem of some kind. Their job, rated by observers or recorded on video, is to use questions which will elicit the facts they need or will focus the

individual's mind in such a way that a clearer account of what he/she is saying will emerge.

☐ Bridging questions

Research work on the structure of counselling sessions — and of conversations in general — has pointed to the fact that these interactions often consist of a series of 'islands'. Individuals talk about one topic for a while, and then pause; at this point, the conversation may either end, or take off in a new direction, which in its own turn will come to a halt sooner or later. In the gaps between such 'islands', skilled counsellors need to be able to recognize that a particular topic has exhausted itself, and should be able to find some means of refocusing attention on a new topic if they want this particular interlude to end and a new departure to take place. Using role-play and video feedback, you can examine your own level of skill in 'bridging' the gaps between islands, by asking questions which will help conversations to embark again after a pause. If you happen to be at a loss for possible things to say to accomplish this, suggestions could again be obtained from other members of your group.

☐ Changing the tone

In some counselling interviews, it may be necessary (in order to achieve the overall purpose of the session) to redirect the subject-matter of an interview in a quite conscious and deliberate way. This can be very difficult if a particular mood pervades the discussion, and would obviously be a wholly inappropriate way to deal with some situations, for example if an individual is expressing a strong emotion (such as grief). One some occasions, however, giving a conversation a gentle and tactful push in a different direction may be the most desirable thing to do.

In this exercise, you are asked to generate lists of possible things you might say in order to

— ask someone, who is already upset, about something else which might upset him or her more, but which needs urgent attention,
— ask someone in a happy or buoyant mood about something important which troubles him/her,
— ask a person who is depressed or anxious some question which might raise his/her spirits by focusing attention on some favourable aspect of his/her life,
— ask someone who has just had bad news, about that news,
— in the middle of a fairly superficial conversation, ask someone a fairly personal question,
— put it to someone whom you think is misleading you or telling lies that you think this is what he/she is doing.

If encounters like these can be carefully reconstructed in role-plays, once again observers and/or video feedback can be used to explore the efficacy of the various questioning tactics used.

Open and closed questions

Many questions that can be asked of individuals invite a simple, yes-or-no answer; others have a larger, but still fairly limited number of possible replies; while others can be answered in a large number of possible ways, with varying degrees of elaboration depending on the mood of the respondent and numerous other factors.

It can be useful, before asking questions in counselling, to think about the kinds of questions they are, and what kinds of responses they permit. Some questions are 'closed'; these can be very useful for information gathering, or for the early stages of counselling when the worker and 'client' do not know each other very well. Closed questions may allow only two possible replies – yes or no; for example the questions

— 'Did you go out last night?'
— 'Are you working at the moment?'

might evoke a lengthy response from listeners but are more likely to meet with a simpler yes-or-no response.

Other closed questions are 'multiple-choice'; in other words the reply, while not likely to be 'yes' or 'no' only, will nevertheless be chosen from a small number of possible alternatives. The questions

— 'What do you usually drink when you go out?'
— 'Where have you tried looking for work?'
— 'How many children have you got?'

are of this type. Questions like this have to be used at some stage during counselling, and are obviously indispensable for assembling factual material and background information about some kinds of problem.

'Open' questions may have an almost unlimited number of responses. They are likely to be most useful when helping individuals to give their views about something, to express their feelings about something, to tell *their* story of some incident, or give *their* account of some problem or situation. They can also be used to obtain individuals' reactions to advice given, or suggestions made by a counsellor. Questions such as

— 'What did you do last night?'
— 'How did you feel when that happened?'
— 'What's your opinion of her?'
— 'How would you react if someone said that to you?'

are all open-ended; clearly, the amount of freedom they allow respondents depends on the exact topic to which they are addressed; but in the main they are liable to be dealt with differently from closed questions on the same issues.

□□ The format for a training exercise on the use of different types of questions follows the same general procedure as that used on other aspects of 'questioning'. First, role-plays of counselling interviews are observed or recorded on video. Second, on playback, a count is made of the number of questions of each type used by the 'counsellor'. Third, individuals discuss whether the questions which were used at various points were of the most appropriate type; or whether other, more useful responses would have been obtained from respondents if a different form of question had been used. Finally, if points such as these *are* recognized, individuals or small groups can generate alternative possible questions, and 'counsellors' can practise using these in subsequent versions of the role-play.

If you would like to transfer your improvements in skills such as questioning to 'real' counselling sessions, you should of course practise the use of different kinds of questions and make note of the kinds of replies they elicit. You can do simple 'experiments' on this by asking people questions in various ways, looking for regularities in their replies, and seeing whether these are related to the way in which the question was asked. This might also help you to establish for yourself the kind of question you feel most comfortable with.

IDENTIFYING FEELINGS

Misunderstandings between people are a fairly common feature of everyday life; language is, to use a famous cliché, a very imperfect medium for communicating messages between one human being and another. The factor which has the strongest influence on how well people communicate is how well they know one another. People who have been close over a long period can sometimes give the impression that they read each other's minds (though there are plenty of examples of the opposite − people who live together for years without ever really getting to know one another). Those who work as helpers are seldom in a position to get to know those whom they help for more than a tiny fraction of their lives, but in this limited period they must get to understand the other person as thoroughly as possible. Helpers should try, therefore, to improve their ability to appreciate other people's states of mind, and a heightened awareness of the means by which people communicate their feelings and intentions ought to be a valuable asset to anyone engaged in counselling work.

The communication of feelings is a very complex aspect of human behaviour: it is achieved by means of spoken language, which is complex enough in itself, and by means of a number of other non-verbal signals including gaze, voice tone, posture, gesture, expressions, dress, and spatial movements. Many variables, such as the age, sex, status, familiarity, or physical size of an individual interact with all these signals and affect how they are perceived by others. From the bewildering array of possible combinations of different kinds of people with different kinds of verbal and non-verbal signals, very few firm rules about communication can be extracted. Would-be counsellors should, however, appraise their own ability to interpret the feelings of others, should at least think about the factors which affect this, and should try to improve their skills in this area if they find themselves seriously at fault. Training exercises like the ones suggested here will not turn prospective helpers into clairvoyants; but they may help them become more attuned to the significance of other people's behaviour as a source of information about the way they feel.

☐☐ Recognizing different emotional states

The first exercise can be used both to help people judge how good they are at recognizing particular emotional states, and to help them learn some of the fairly well-established 'cues' which are associated with those states. This exercise and the others which follow are based on research work in the area of non-verbal communication.

	Facial expression	Posture	Gestures	Voice tone
Anxiety/fear	Eyebrows and eyelids raised; mouth open, lips and side of mouth drawn back	Body tense, legs closed	Fidgeting, small uncontrolled movements	Voice shaky, pitch high
Depression	Jaw loose, eyes narrowed, skin between eyebrows furrowed; corners of mouth turned down	Body hung forward, shoulders low, head down; body turned away from addressee	Hands and arms loose; limp hand movements	Low pitch, slow pace, long pauses
Hostility	Mouth sealed firmly or teeth bared; eyes level and staring steadily	Body erect and tense; directly facing addressee	Arms open; firm movements of hands, possibly pointing of fingers	Voice steady, even emphasis given to each word

This research has suggested that, amongst the very large number of emotions that can be conveyed through different combinations of facial expressions, there are six basic emotions of which the others can be viewed as compounds or variations: happiness, sadness, fear, anger, surprise, and disgust. Linked to these there are also changes in other indicators like bodily movements, gestures, and tone of voice. The table on the previous page lists some of the characteristics associated with three emotions with which counsellors are likely to be confronted. A list like this can be extended to cover a large number of emotional states, but it should be borne in mind that for many emotions the signals which people use to judge them may not be as consistent as those suggested here. Information of the kind shown in the table can be used in a number of exercises.

Individuals who feel doubtful about their ability to identify some of the main emotional signals can be shown a series of photographs. They can make a simple assessment of their own ability to identify feelings on the basis of the number they recognize correctly. Alternatively, instead of photographs, other group members can portray the emotions – though the success of this would depend on the ability of the actors to 'mimic' the required expressions.

Taking one photograph at a time, try to generate as many adjectives as possible which you think describe the feeling expressed by the face; you can do this on your own or in company with other members of your group (in which case you can compare your lists to see how much overlap there is).

It is not uncommon for people to realize that someone is in such-and-such a mood, but to misjudge completely the extent of the person's feelings. Another exercise might therefore be to take a number of photographs, like those shown below, and to rank-order them according to the *strength* of a particular feeling they exhibit.

Finally, you can expand on the table on page 79 by compiling a list of the signals associated with other emotions you have experienced or observed. If you are working in a pair or a group you can also explore the degree to which people agree that a particular signal is connected with a particular emotional state. Other dimensions, such as gaze, spatial movements, or feature of speech may also be included for this purpose.

☐ Silent video

A further exercise on the recognition of different emotions can be carried out using video. Working in pairs, individuals are asked to role-play a counselling session in which the counsellee expresses a particular feeling to the helper. The camera should focus for the most part on the behaviour of the former. The feelings or situations used can be drawn from a prearranged list (compiled by a tutor or by one group member alone). The video sequences are then played back without sound, to see whether *on the basis of the non-verbal components alone* observers can identify the kinds of feelings being expressed.

'Influencing' skills

Helping others is an activity which involves a great deal of responsibility; people in need of help look upon those whom they have asked for it, or whose appointed task it is to help them, in a special frame of mind. The helper's reaction to the situation is crucial in determining its outcome. It can lead to complete 'success' in terms of the solution of a problem or the undertaking of personal change, or it can have completely the opposite effect – of making matters worse, creating new problems, and even robbing individuals of whatever motivation to change they might have had beforehand.

It is therefore very important that would-be helpers should be aware of the effects their words and actions can have upon others. They should be able to judge as finely as possible the likely ramifications of any decision they take, or the likely responses that will be evoked when they deal with other people in any particular way. Potential helpers should also not mislead themselves into believing that they can engage in counselling without at some point committing themselves and *doing something*. Helpers must acknowledge that at some stage they are certain to influence what the person with the problem does – even if they had been struggling to maintain a 'low profile' and 'intervene' as little as possible.

Trying to induce people with problems into doing the bulk of the work themselves is a totally acceptable helping strategy. It will be more valuable still if it is also accompanied by an attempt to help individuals develop *self-help* skills which they can deploy when future problems arise. But in some contexts such an approach will just not work. People want to be given suggestions as to what to do about their problems. They want to be, if not directed, at least supported, prodded into action, or cajoled into a better frame of mind. A 'non-interventionist' tactic will invite rancour in circumstances like this, just as the molly-coddling approach of other schools of helping can create dependency or an exploitative attitude on the part of those on the receiving end.

The best solution to all of these difficulties is to be aware of yourself; to have at your disposal a number of different strategies that can be called into play as and when necessary; to have a measured sense of which effects are liable to flow from which actions you take at any given point; and to have the skills of putting across what you want to put across, clearly and accurately, in a way that accords with your own approach to your work. The exercises in this section are intended to help individuals to develop skills of these kinds.

These exercises alone will not, however, produce changes in counselling skill; those who wish to make perceptible improvements in their ability to counsel must be constantly implementing what they have learnt in training sessions and testing its viability in real helping encounters. Where possible, individuals should 'transfer' their skills to situations in which they are actively working with others: on placements if they are on training courses, with selected cases if they are already at work, with friends who have problems if there are no opportunities like the former available to them. To make this even more effective, individuals should consider keeping a log of the kinds of things they do, the context, and the results. This will enable them to build up a fuller picture of their own skills development, map out exactly which exercises seem to have worked or not to have worked for them, and identify any areas that seem to need further practice and improvement.

INFORMATION GIVING

One basic skill which a good helper ought to possess is that of giving information. To most people the passing on of facts is a fairly straightforward business; in the context of helping, however, it needs to be done with a little more care, and the worker must to a certain extent employ skills that are perhaps usually thought of as more the domain of the teacher than that of the counsellor. In addition, there is a tendency for many helpers to move at once to the emotional side of people's problems, when a mere imparting of the facts about local housing, rights, courtroom procedure, or whatever would be all that is required. Finally, there is more than one way to convey information; and workers in the helping field often have a very limited view of the means they can use to get vital information across to those who need it to solve their problems. The first batch of exercises in this section is therefore devoted to the fostering of informational or 'teaching' skills.

☐☐ **Face-to-face**
Most information given as part of a helping encounter will be exchanged between the worker and his/her client on a one-to-one or small group basis. The skills of putting information across can also be practised in this context.

☐ Ask each member of your group to give a talk to the remainder of the group on one topic on which he/she feels qualified to speak. This might be a hobby or pastime, an account of an experience, an outline of the basic facts pertaining to any subject in which he/she is interested. The talk, lasting not more than five minutes, should have as high an information content as possible, and be presented in as clear, logical, and easily remembered a manner as possible. Other group members can then comment on what they have learned and on the overall delivery of the talk as a 'mini-lecture'. As an alternative this exercise can be conducted in pairs with each individual relaying information to the other in turn.

☐ The exercise can then be made more difficult by asking group members to find, collect, and prepare some facts on less familiar topics. A series of subjects are listed on cards and drawn from a hat by group members. Each has then to prepare a five-minute talk as before, but will this time have to search out some relevant information, think about it a little more, and spend more time organizing it into a form in which it can be digested by others. While the previous exercise can be carried out in a single session or part of a session, this exercise will be spread over two group meetings, with time for information search and preparation in between.

☐☐ Visual aids

Not all information is communicated face-to-face; most of the information we receive nowadays is in printed or broadcast form. The use of the printed word and of the media can also be practised by individuals and groups.

☐ Information leaflets

Much of the information required by people with problems comes to them in leaflet form. All too often, this diet of essential facts is more liable to constipate than nourish those for whom it is designed; official attempts at information giving have often been referred to as 'gobbledegook' (Vernon 1980). A valuable exercise in information giving might be to take an official leaflet that falls into this category, and rewrite it in a form in which it can be more easily understood by those to whom it is addressed – without losing any of the actual information content. This should tax your imagination in finding alternatives to jargon.

But there are also many points on which people with problems require information, where the facts are just not available to them in any form. Another version of this exercise would therefore be to make a list of topics like these, and prepare an information leaflet on one or more of them that would fill the gap which exists.

☐ Information video tapes

A more vivid means of putting information across, which can also be useful in work with groups, is the video tape recorder. If the members of a training group can be given access to such a machine, they could be asked to make short (say five-minute) 'information tapes' designed to transmit as much information as possible, in as attractive a form as possible, to a particular target group. To do this, a list of topics is first assembled (for example aspects of tenants' rights; child care; local job opportunities; the procedure in tribunals; supplementary benefits; leisure amenities; mental health law). Having chosen one topic, the group then collects and selects some facts to put across on video; develops some ideas for doing so in a lively, engaging way; and records the tape perhaps with some graphics to illustrate various points. If you have access to an editing machine, the possibilities of making longer and more professional productions will soon become apparent.

□□ Doing your own PR

On other occasions, information will be compiled and prepared in the hope that it will reach a larger audience. If helpers decide that they would like to run a group; if they want to advertise the availability of a particular service; if they are showing films, trying to run a campaign, or doing anything for which they hope to attract the attention of people in need of help whom they might not otherwise meet, they will need to consider how best to go about this.

□ Once again, writing an information leaflet which will be distributed to various individuals and groups would be a worthwhile exercise in this respect. Another exercise would be to design a poster announcing some event, conveying some information, or making some kind of invitation to interested parties within a certain area. Imagine that you and the members of your group are involved in some activity of this type and have to produce an A2-size poster that will incorporate the necessary information in as eye-catching a design as possible.

□ Press release. As a further development of this, group members can also be asked to imagine that they have to write a one-page statement for release to the local press, communicating some important facts or putting forward a case on some controversial issue. The statement might be an announcement of the opening of a new day centre or other facility; the start of a campaign; a summary of some facts that would be of value to local tenants, old people, parents of young children, or whatever. It will have to be written with a certain finesse if it is to hold the attention of newspaper sub-editors. The skills of assembling, condensing, and expressing facts in a direct, clear, and appealing way can all be practised in an exercise of this kind. If you are able to do so, you could even invite a local newspaper 'copy-taster' along to judge your efforts in this respect.

While for most workers in the helping professions the majority of the instances in which they have to convey information will be of the face-to-face variety, the exercises in relating information to a wider public should not only help them extend these skills but might also enhance their abilities in one-to-one teaching in addition.

Information giving is a component of counselling the importance of which has been considerably underestimated in the past. Teaching obviously involves many other skills than the sheer giving of information and cannot be dealt with at any length here (those who would like to find out more about teaching skills should consult some of the books cited at the end of this chapter). For the present, we turn to some skills more commonly regarded as essential parts of the counselling process.

SELF-DISCLOSURE

One way to get individuals to talk about themselves, to reinforce a relationship with them, and to give them indirect advice by way of illustration, is to tell them things about yourself. This is known as 'self-disclosure' and it has been shown that self-disclosing statements made by one person to another tend to elicit similar self-disclosures from the other person. A number of exercises can be carried out to help individuals examine their own degree of self-disclosure, and to practise using self-disclosure as a device in counselling sessions.

☐ Self-referring statements

One comparatively simple exercise that can be conducted in small groups is to ask individuals to monitor the extent to which other members of the group use self-disclosing statements in typical counselling sessions. To do this you may need to set up a role-play recreating a helping session – perhaps along the lines suggested above (p. 66).

The observer's task in this case is to make a count of the number of statements the 'counsellor' makes which involve a reference to him/herself; to further subdivide these into statements which refer to self in various ways, focusing special attention on statements in which the counsellor reveals something to the person being helped. Examples of such statements are:

— 'I've been in this situation myself. What happened was . . .'
— 'I know exactly how you feel – the same thing happened to me.'
— 'I remember once I . . .'
— 'Whenever people say things like that to me I always feel . . .'

Such statements may be followed by personal anecdotes; revelations of inner feelings or attitudes; or just by supportive acknowledgements that the helper has experiences which correspond to or overlap with those of the person being helped.

☐ Taking responsibility

Another difference which can be monitored in the same way is the extent to which, when individuals express views or make statements about attitudes of some kind, they do so in a way which refers the matter to themselves; in other words, they set out their own views on an issue, or make it clear that a particular view is theirs rather than derived from elsewhere. For example, there is a difference between saying 'I think that such-and-such is the case', and attributing the ownership of the attitude or belief to someone else – like the agency, society in general, or other people specific to an individual case. Appraise each other's performance in role-plays to see how far individuals use 'owned' statements or statements which attribute beliefs to others when making arguments of any kind.

Self-disclosure to others

It can be useful to ask yourself to what extent you are willing to tell other people particular things about yourself, by examining the amount of information about you that other people, in specific categories, possess. Some people have only a few intimate acquaintances; others have a wide circle of friends with whom they may share a great many revelations about what others would regard as very personal affairs. Individuals can assess this aspect of their 'social selves' by doing this exercise.

□□ First of all, ask group members to make a long list (which they can keep to themselves) of a whole range of aspects of themselves — or *kinds* of attributes if they would rather not write down the specifics. These might range, for example, from information about their jobs, cars, or houses, through facts about their families, their bank balances, their love affairs, political views, moral or religious

Information about your	*Would you reveal it to*
Job	A complete stranger on a train
Car	A stranger to whom you've been
Home	introduced at a work meeting
Family	A stranger to whom you've been
How children are doing at school	introduced at a party
A problem one family member	A very casual acquaintance
has	Someone of lower status at work
A previous illness	Someone of higher status at work
A recent loss/failure you	A work colleague with whom
experienced	you're on good terms but never
Fantasies with reference to	mix with socially
Work	A friend (not close)
Politics	A close friend
Sex	One of your children
Political views	One of your parents
Morals	Your boy-friend/girl-friend/
Religious beliefs	husband/wife
Marriage	
Previous sex life or love affairs	
Ambitions	
Innermost thoughts	

beliefs, or most secret desires, to very personal ideas or feelings which they may never have shared with anyone.

Alternatively, ask them to rate a series of items in terms of how 'revealing' they are of self (items are given in the box).

Second, ask them to make a long list of different categories of people, from the public and official to the intimate and closely related. This could cover a list of types that you give to them, or could be done on an entirely open-ended basis.

Third, now ask them to think about which of the sorts of people they have listed they would be happy to tell some of the different kinds of facts they have listed about themselves previously. Compare the responses of different group members and their reasons for giving the facts that they do. Finally, ask them to think in particular about which kinds of things they would be willing to reveal in a counselling situation if they believed it would enhance the warmth of it or otherwise help it along.

Of course, circumstances also play an important part in how much we will reveal to others and you can add another layer of interest to the exercise by asking people to specify various kinds of contexts in which they would and would not reveal specific kinds of information to specifie kinds of people.

Once again, you might find it worthwhile to try out some simple 'experiments' to gauge whether the things you have tried in training sessions actually work in real life. Try out 'self-disclosure' when talking to others and see if it elicits disclosures from them. *Don't* do this of course if it's going to make you or them feel uncomfortable.

Promoting self-disclosure

Individuals may decide, on the basis of exercises like the above, that they do not wish to 'use themselves' in this way during counselling. This is of course absolutely at their discretion and no pressure whatever should be put upon them to alter this. If on the other hand they would like to make use of self-disclosures in helping but are uncertain how to, some brief training exercises can be introduced.

☐ In one, role-plays are set up in which the 'helpee' makes a statement of some kind about a problem which he/she has. The counsellor's tasks is then to:

(a) respond with something in his/her experience which is appropriate to what has been said; *or* find a way of saying that this is *not* in his/her experience — both without losing the momentum of the conversation; and
(b) redirect attention, the focus of the conversation, back to the speaker; in such a way that he/she feels encouraged to explore the problem in more depth.

Observers should then comment on how well this was done, what improvements might be made, and so on.

RESPONDING TO AND COMMUNICATING FEELINGS

Many of the problems which have to be dealt with by counselling are emotional in nature. Even if this were not the case, most other kinds of problems which people experience evoke some kinds of feelings in them – of anxiety, disappointment, frustration, or annoyance for example. As well as being able to recognize such feelings, good counsellors should also be able to respond to them in a helpful, appropriate way; and should in addition be able to convey their own feelings to individuals as part of an honest – and useful – response to their problems.

□□ Responses to feelings

You can conduct exercises on this in a small group, by asking individuals to make lists of possible responses they might make to expressions of feeling of various kinds. For example, group members produce a list of five possible things to say in response to an *angry* statement, an *anxious* statement, a statement of *suspicion*, a statement about *feelings of inferiority*, and so on. This would be more useful however if the feelings to which they had to respond were made more concrete and given more detail. For instance, group members could be invited to generate a list of five possible things to say to the following:

— A young man who has failed to get a job he wanted very much.
— A friend who has had his/her wallet or purse stolen; it contained £50.
— A mother of three whose oldest boy seems to have run away; she is both very worried and very angry.
— A middle-aged man or woman who is still in considerable grief eighteen months after the death of his/her spouse.
— A teenager who is feeling guilty or ashamed about having injured a pedestrian in a cycling accident.

Items like these can easily be made more 'real' if they are embellished with detail by some group members for the benefit of others. In addition to generating lists of responses and discussing the relative value of each, the exercise can also be augmented using role-play, video, and feedback as in other exercises outlined above.

An extension of this exercise is for group members to think about one person whose problems they are concerned with at the moment. Each member produces one 'case' in this way which might be a friend or relative, or someone with whom they are working on a placement, or someone recalled from the past. Individuals can then either:

(a) *imagine* a situation in which this individual expressed a particular feeling; remember the response that was made; make a list of possible alternative responses; and/or describe the situation to the rest of the group to see what responses *other* group members would have made; or

(b) *role-play* the part of the individual in front of other group members, inviting them to give responses they would have given under the circumstances.

In this way, group members can develop a range of possible replies that might be made to emotionally loaded statements of different kinds. This would almost certainly include some ideas that would not have occurred to them at the time. If need be, group members can practise or rehearse some of these in further specially constructed role-plays.

Reflection

Another vital aspect of the counsellor's ability to respond to an individual's feelings in a suitable manner is the capacity to show individuals that you understand the way they are feeling by, as it were, *reflecting* their feelings back to them in words and expressions. To an extent this can be regarded as a skill of 'attending' rather than of influence, but in so far as it does have an important effect on the subsequent course of counselling we discuss it here.

If you have ever expressed a problem to someone who then stared at you blankly or whose response suggested that he or she had not understood a word you said, you will probably appreciate the importance of reflection. Accurate reflection encourages individuals to continue talking about their problems and to explore them, and give an account of them in more depth.

☐ Paraphrase

At the simplest level the ability to 'reflect' is anchored in the ability to repeat what someone has said using a different form of words. People would obviously think you highly peculiar if you repeated their exact words; try this and see. In this exercise individuals, working in pairs, make statements to each other. The addressee's task in each case is to find a way of saying what the speaker has said, using different words, but which conveys exactly the same meaning as the speaker's statement. For example speakers might say:

— 'Last week things seemed to go wrong one thing after another. Every day something new happened I hadn't been ready for. I really had a run of bad luck — by the end of the week I was a nervous wreck.'

— 'Going to the Jobcentre's a complete waste of time. They never have anything. Looking in the papers is just as bad. You always think it's worth a try but then when you look you realize you shouldn't have bothered.'

The listener must in each case try to relate back to the speaker the same basic message but expressed in a different way. With a small amount of thought pairs of individuals will be able to make up statements like these for their partners to paraphrase; try making them progressively more difficult each time.

☐ Mirroring and 'mood-matching'

Paraphrasing is sometimes referred to as 'reflection of content'. Much more difficult is the business of reflecting feelings. Obviously reflecting contents is a part of this, but other means must be used to convey the emotional component of expressions.

One way of doing this is for individuals, this time again working in trios, to try to convey feelings to each other by non-verbal means − that is by means of facial expressions, voice tone, and so forth. The recipient's objective in this case is to behave as if he/she were a mirror: to reflect, as accurately as possible, the feelings the first person is expressing. The third member of the trio acts as an observer and comments on (or rates) the accuracy of the mirroring. If people don't do too well at this, they could use some of the information in the table on p. 79 (and information from other sources quoted at the end of this chapter) to practise their skills in front of a *real* mirror at home.

This exercise can be used to look both at momentary feelings − fleeting instances of anger or worry − and at moods − more drawn-out experiences of anxiety or depression.

☐ General and particular feelings

Another way to improve reflecting skills is to try first of all to identify the feeling a person is expressing and to *verbalize it* to yourself before reflecting it, rather than trying to mirror the person's facial expressions or movements. In doing this it can be helpful to move from a 'general' emotional label, such as 'angry' or 'unhappy', to more specialized labels like furious, annoyed, or bitter; or miserable, gloomy, or fed-up. Individuals might find it worthwhile, in approaching the skills of reflection in this way, to make a list of word labels for different feelings, and see how they are interrelated − which are specific forms of others, which are admixtures of other kinds of feeling, etc. Some word labels for emotions are given in the check-list.

☐ Practising reflection

Finally, the skill of reflection can be assessed and practised in a full-scale role-play of a counselling interview along the lines suggested earlier in this chapter. In carrying out role-plays of this kind, 'counsellors' should bear in mind − and observers should look for − some of the important ingredients of reflection of feeling. These are first, that the individual's emotional state should be directly labelled in the response; second, that there should be a direct personal reference to the individual in the response; and third, it should be made clear that the counsellor appreciates the individual's feelings *at that moment*; in other words, his/her attention is focused on the individual *now*.

Empathy and support

Showing an individual that you understand his or her feelings is one important aspect of a counsellor's response. A skill that is equally important in effective counselling is that of conveying *empathy*, or the impression that you not only comprehend another person's feelings, but also share them to some extent. In some cases this may need to take the form of *expressing active support* for an individual, either by endorsing a statement of feeling or opinion, or by communicating sympathy, warmth, or encouragement.

Affect word check-list

Happy	Sad	Excited	Angry
Surprised	Depressed	Hysterical	Furious
Overjoyed	Gloomy	Panicky	Annoyed
Cheerful	Dismayed	Unsettled	Irritated
Buoyant	Disappointed	Anxious	Tetchy
Merry	Deflated	Curious	Aggrieved
Proud	Ashamed	Suspicious	Jealous
Satisfied	Guilty	Frustrated	Defeated
Content	Lost	Determined	Vicious
Mellow	Helpless	Tenacious	Vengeful
Serene	Grief-stricken	Disgusted	Cheated
Light-hearted	Miserable	Afraid	Rejected
Light-headed	Dejected	Terrified	Downcast
Triumphant	Disdainful	Apprehensive	Woeful
Carefree	Aloof	Self-righteous	Crushed
Tender	Scornful	Vindicated	Foolish
Loving	Concerned	Ridiculous	Trapped
Sympathetic	Worried	Sorrowful	Cold-blooded
Relieved	Sorry	Mischievous	Sullen
Glad	Pained	Silly	Haughty
Ecstatic	Humiliated	Humorous	Confused
Grateful	Used	Mortified	Defiant
Pleased	Remorseful	Bored	Resentful
Delighted	Indifferent	Bashful	Peeved
Amused	Forgiving	Hostile	Churlish

☐☐ 'Feeling' words

The box above contains a list of words which can be used to describe emotions and emotional states. One way to develop the capacity to convey empathy is to conjure up the experience of different emotions and a check-list of 'affect' words like the one shown here can be used as the basis for this.

Individuals should be asked to survey this list, or part of it, or another list similar to it, and see whether they can answer a number of questions for themselves. These might include:

1 Which of the feelings in this list have you ever experienced?
2 Which have you not experienced but think you have seen in others?
3 Select five or six of the words in the list. What kinds of things do you think would have to happen to people to make them feel this way? See if you can list half-a-dozen events or circumstances that would produce each feeling in turn.
4 Select five or six of the words which describe feelings you have had at some time.

   (a) Think about the events or circumstances that were associated with each in turn.
   (b) Think about something you would have liked someone to say to you at the time, or which you think would have helped you if the feeling was a bad one, or made you feel even better if the feeling was a good one. Make a list of six things for each feeling in turn.

5 Make a list of three or four people you know at present or have known in the past. Think of one problem which each person has or has had. Which words on the check-list describe the feelings these individuals probably have (or had)? Which of these feelings have you experienced yourself?
6 If possible take five or six words from the list which describe feelings you have never had. What kinds of events or experiences do you think would make you have these feelings?

The outcomes of any or all of these introspections can be kept by individuals to themselves; can be shared with one other person in peer interviews; or can be pooled together with those of several others in a small group discussion. The objective in each case is to help individuals appraise the boundaries of their own experience; to help them appreciate the qualities of different emotions as a basis of empathy training; and to increase their understanding of how individuals in different emotional states are likely to react when spoken to in various ways.

☐ Empathy 'training'
The foregoing exercise can be used as the starting-point for another concerned with the development of empathy. Here, individuals are asked to use fantasy to place themselves in the position of other people in imaginary social situations.

These situations must however be based on reality. Give the members of your group a general description of a social encounter, for example:

— Trying to help someone who is worrying a lot to be more relaxed.
— Helping someone who feels very negative about him/herself to feel more positive.
— Helping someone who is shy or unconfident to mix more with others.
— Trying to help someone in an unhappy relationship to do something about it.

and are asked to think of one specific instance of such problems which is known to them personally. They are then invited to 'fantasize' about this individual's problems — to imagine incidents in which he/she is involved, to recreate as vividly as possible in their minds various things that have happened, and to allow the imagination to wander over the various other possibilities that might occur. Each group member then describes his/her fantasy to the rest of the group; giving details of the feelings, thoughts, and behaviour of each person involved in the fantasy, and describing how various incidents looked from different participants' points of view. Listening group members are asked to place themselves, in imagination, in the position of each participant in turn. In this way individuals learn a little of how it might feel to be in the stance of others in a variety of difficult social situations.

☐ Points of view

As an alternative to this exercise, or as a means of making it more lifelike, group members take part in brief role-plays in which participants are at odds with each other because of their views of and feelings about the situation in question. Participants in the role-plays must first be given 'briefs' which outline their starting-points for action; for example, the actors in a three-cornered role-play might be given simple sketches like the ones shown below. (With a larger group, several three-person role-plays could be conducted simultaneously, or other members could act as observers.)

☐ Person 1

You are a teenage boy or girl who has been missing school a great deal. You find school very boring, and in any case you haven't been doing too well at it over the past eighteen months or so and you don't think you can keep up with it any more. The education welfare officer has come round to see your mother (who is separated from your father); he wants to know why you're not attending school. Your mother can get into trouble because you don't go to school. You can be sent to a special school for truants. You don't care about not going back to school, but you don't want your mother to get into trouble and you would be willing to go to the other school if that would sort things out.

☐ Person 2

You are the mother of a teenage boy or girl who has been missing school a lot recently. The education welfare officer has arrived to look into the case. You can't understand your child's attitude any more. A couple of years ago he/she was doing very well at school, got good marks, and seemed quite happy. After your marriage broke up things seemed to change for the child and you feel guilty about his/her problems since then. Still you don't want your son/daughter to go to a special school or a truancy centre. You would like help for him/her to sort out his/her problems. You believe a move would do more damage.

☐ Person 3

You are an education welfare officer. You have come to see the mother of a child who has been truanting a great deal. You want to understand the reasons for the child's behaviour but you tend to the view that the child will almost certainly have to be sent to a truancy centre.

After beginning a role-play using these prompts and running it for about five minutes, the organizer should stop the action and ask people to write down:

(1) how they are feeling;
(2) how other participants are feeling;
(3) Why they think the others are saying what they're saying and behaving as they're behaving.

Discussion might then be focused on the similarities and differences between the various participants' points of view; whether these are reconcilable or not; and in particular, on how accurate each actor's perception is of the feelings of his/her peers. Although each individual is pursuing a different goal in this role-play, the way in which each one is doing so will be dependent on his/her level of understanding of the feelings and views of the other two participants. Once again, their appreciation of the viewpoints of others − their degree of empathy − can be enhanced by weighing up the gulfs that may exist between their perspectives and those of others; and by discussing the reasons why these gulfs exist and the ways in which they might take them into account in a 'real' situation of this type.

There are of course many other encounters which can be set up, role-played, and discussed in this way.

☐ Role-reversal

A similar exercise to the preceding one can also be built on role-reversal, an extension of the exercises described previously (p. 62). Here, in addition to comparing the perspectives of different actors in a role-play, the exercise also forces you to a certain extent to adopt these perspectives by asking you to play different parts at different times. This will be at its most useful if two partners are given adversary or conflicting roles; if they are given briefs (like the ones just illustrated) which put them at odds with each other. 'Prompts' of this kind can be written for pairs such as:

— A husband and wife whose marriage is in difficulties.
— A parent and child having an argument about dress.
— Two parents arguing over whether a child should be punished, one taking a lenient and the other a disciplinarian point of view.
— Two people arguing about how money should be spent — one for thriftiness and the other for 'living it up'.

After the incumbents have played one role for a few minutes, the role-play is halted and the roles reversed; when a few more minutes have elapsed, the duo discuss the kinds of counters they gave to each other's arguments (when playing each role in turn), the way they felt in each role, and whether they have learnt anything about their initial adversary's point of view. As before, this can be used to bring out important similarities and differences which may develop each person's understanding of (and empathy with) the position of the other.

☐ Giving support
One other exercise which can be used as part of an 'empathy training' sequence is the simple observation of role-plays in which counsellors are asked to express support to individuals with emotional problems of various kinds. Using the now-familiar two-person role-play format (with observers) attention can be directed specifically at the use of supporting statements by counsellors, at their verbal and non-verbal skill, and at the relative merits of different kinds of 'empathic' response for dealing with problems of various sorts. This exercise and all of the preceding ones on empathy will prove most valuable if individuals' diverse approaches to them are discussed as fully as possible after each role-playing interlude.

Conveying feelings

Empathy is however only one — though admittedly a very important one — of the many feelings counsellors might wish to put across during helping sessions. Exercises similar in structure to that just described on 'giving support' could be repeated for almost any kind of feeling which one person might wish to convey to another as a way of helping him or her with a problem.

☐☐ An alternative route to the development of skill in the communication of feelings might employ a more game-like exercise which is complementary to some of the methods suggested earlier on the theme of 'responding to feelings'.

This exercise is concerned principally with the non-verbal aspects of emotional expression. Group members depict — using facial expressions, gestures, or posture and movement — a number of different emotions, to see whether an 'audience' (consisting of other group members) can identify the feeling they are trying to convey. Several cards or pieces of paper are prepared which have abbreviated descriptions of emotional states written or typed on them, for example:

Anger. You have just opened a letter which informs you that someone with whom you had a collision in your car a few weeks ago — and whose fault the accident was — is not covered by insurance.
Sadness. Some close friends have just told you that they have decided to emigrate to Australia and you realize you will miss them a lot.
Happiness/pleasure. You have just had a phone call saying that you have got a job you really wanted.
Disgust. You have just read a newspaper account of the recovery of bodies following a major air disaster.
Fear. You are in the waiting room in a hospital expecting to be called any moment to get the results of some medical tests.
Surprise. It is your birthday and, unexpectedly, a number of friends who live some distance away turn up to help you celebrate.

The cards or pieces of paper are put in a hat and picked at random by volunteer members of the group. Remaining group members assess the quality of the 'performances' given by the volunteers and comment on the signals by which different emotions can be conveyed. More complex feelings and more complex descriptions can be used if group members want to take the exercise further; three sub-groups might be formed, each one in turn producing some emotion cards which the second group has to express to the third.

The idea which underlies all of the exercises in this section is not that of turning people into better actors. The overall aim is to help individuals discover whether there is a congruence between what they think they are putting across to others and what is actually going across. If there is a gap between the impression they think they are giving and the impression others are in fact receiving, they can use the exercises to find out more about the communication of emotional meaning and to improve their skills in the necessary ways.

As with all other exercises, those wishing to make real improvements in their counselling skills must also take things a step further: they must try them out in day-to-day practice, in encounters with people whom they are trying to help, and perhaps even more widely in the rest of their dealings with others. The only way to be sure you have improved your ability in a particular area is to try out your skills in your work and see if they have the desired effect.

Persuasion and influence

People with problems often find themselves in a weak position in relation to others. They may be worried, frustrated, or confused, may be tired from lack of sleep, or their confidence may be at a low ebb as a result of the difficulties they are facing. In addition, those with problems may regard professional helpers as more 'educated' than themselves; differences in social class, age, or other factors, coupled with the fact that the worker may often be housed in a large office block protected by layers of other workers, may make the helpee see the helper as someone of higher status than him- or herself. While amongst some people who come to helping agencies all of this evokes complete mistrust and disrespect, for the most part helpers tend to be in a position of dominance over those whom they are assigned to help.

Some people quite rightly see grave dangers in the position of relative power in which professional helpers find themselves. Their advice is likely to be heeded even when wrong; they may simply reinforce the differences in life chances between themselves and their clients; and may even exploit the helping relationship to gratify their own personal needs for limited power or a misplaced expression of altruism.

For this reason, the direct giving of advice or the exertion of personal influence is looked at askance in many approaches to counsellor training. They favour instead a 'non-directive' strategy in which the counsellor places the onus for solving problems and making decisions entirely in the hands of the individual whose problems are under discussion. A large proportion of the time such an approach does seem to be most effective; individuals are forced to think for themselves, and help themselves, and by feeling at the end that the result is based on their own efforts are much more likely to be able to solve their own problems in the future. In some cases, however, the worker must be able and willing to advise and persuade, and to wield personal influence. Some individuals simply cannot progress without external direction and welcome suggestions that are made to them. Others, who may be responsive most of the time to non-directive help, may occasionally reach an impasse from which only an outside agent can extricate them. And in other instances, people may elect for courses of action from which they clearly have to be dissuaded because of the probable effects on themselves, their families, or their friends.

Perhaps the most important aspect of influencing to appreciate in relation to the helping process is *when* it is happening. Many statements of opinion or attempts to control others are harmful because they are not recognizable. Labelling an opinion or an effort to persuade as such will rob it of most of its potential dangers. Used with skill and discretion such activities need not make individuals any more dependent on helpers than friends become when they seek a word of advice from each other. Helpers should therefore learn to be aware, first, of moments when they themselves are inclined to slip into an advice-giving 'mode' (perhaps inadvertently); and, second, of moments in counselling when the giving of advice or the use of persuasive argument might be appropriate.

ADVICE GIVING

The notion of advice is at the core of the concept of counselling; helping individuals to see the most suitable course of action to take *vis-à-vis* some problem is the largest single component of what the verb 'to counsel' denotes. Used properly, however, the giving of advice would occur only after lengthy consideration by the counsellor and the individual with the problem of all the options available.

The exercises here, as elsewhere in this book, are addressed not to the *what* of advising – not to the kinds of advice that should be given to people with particular kinds of difficulty – but to the *how*. They are concerned, in other words, with the *skill* of effectively giving a certain piece of advice once a decision to give it has been reached.

☐☐ Advice giving can be explored and practised in role-plays in several ways. First, individuals can be presented with various problems, such as those listed in the counselling exercise earlier in this chapter (p. 63), and asked to respond to them with a piece of advice – that is, with a positive, concrete suggestion as to a course of action that might be taken concerning the problem, or with a proposal that entails some kind of active approach towards problem solution. Observers should, in commenting on the counsellor's performance, pay more attention to the manner in which the advice is given, its likelihood of being accepted, the way in which it is expressed, and so on, than to the actual content.

☐ A second exercise on advice giving focuses instead on the best way in which certain kinds of advice ought to be phrased, in order to increase the chances that their recipients will follow them. This applies particularly to situations in which the advice involves a course of action that is likely to present difficulties for an individual, for example:

— Someone who is afraid of what he/she might find out about his/her symptoms is advised to see a doctor.
— An individual who has just admitted a fairly serious offence to the counsellor is advised that it is in his/her best interests to go to the police.
— A tense or worried person is given advice about taking things more easily, about relaxing, or about controlling his/her feelings of anxiety.
— An individual who is having a major problem with someone else (e.g. at work, in marriage) and who is afraid to broach the subject with that person is advised that this is the only realistic course of action.

Participants in this exercise should be able to embellish these examples, possibly with realistic details taken from their own experience, and thereby make the exercise more lifelike. Like other exercises this one can be run either in groups of three, in which one person acts as counsellor, another presents the problem, and a third observes; or in a large-group format, where a single pair is observed by the other members of the group. Either way, observation and discussion should focus on the way in which advice is put across, the counsellor's use of eye contact and other non-verbal signals to reinforce his/her message, and the way in which he/she pursues the line of advice and supports it with subsidiary arguments.

This exercise is based on the assumption that in the imaginary situation on which the role-play is based, the advice being given really is the best possible under the circumstances. If having set up a role-play participants feel there are other courses of action they would like to suggest, the advice giving should be focused on these instead.

As far as this last point is concerned, the relative value of different kinds of advice should obviously be appraised within the context of exercises like the ones set out here. Although this book is primarily, as mentioned above, about the *how* of counselling, training in this area cannot ignore the *what* entirely and any attempt to do this will be to the detriment of individuals' helping skills. A third exercise on advice giving can be conducted in which one group member at a time takes a problem (real or imaginary, his/her own or someone else's) to the rest of the group. The individual concerned should preferably sit in the centre of the group. He/she first outlines the problem to the whole group and then invites suggestions as to what he/she should do about it. Group members then throw in suggestions as they occur to them. As different ideas are proposed in this way, the person with the problem gives a general indication of his/her immediate reaction to the advice – and of whether or not it might be useful for actually solving the problem. For each 'problem' presented in this way, a list of the most fruitful suggestions can be drawn up and displayed on the wall for future reference.

PERSUASION EXERCISES

Advice is a form of persuasion. Although we usually assume that 'advising' means arguing for one of a number of alternatives open to the person with the problem, the skill of advising effectively is very similar (from an interactive point of view) to the skills of persuading, encouraging, and inducing. An equally important skill for those who are helping with other people's problems is that of resisting persuasion. All of these can be developed using exercises like those outlined below, which have two inter-related aims:

1 To help individuals acquire the ability to approach delicate or emotive topics in a rational manner; and
2 To develop individuals' abilities of persuading others or of resisting pressure applied to them.

□□ In the simplest 'persuasion exercise', a group is organized so that its members have to try to convince each other of their own points of view on some topic. In an initial run of this kind of exercise, the topics used can range over many areas beyond those of helping as such, and can include politics, morals, or any other areas of argument and controversy. Participants can be given a set of instructions like those shown in the box below.

You have a point of view on a given topic.

1 Set out this point of view as clearly as you can. Think it through, and write it down if necessary.
2 Put it across to someone else (or to a group), setting yourself a time limit of two minutes for this. Marshall as many arguments as you can for your point of view and make them as convincingly as possible.
3 Take a count at the end of any group members who still disagree with you and list their reasons for doing so *or* if you are working with one person only, list any reasons he/she gives for not endorsing your point of view.
4 Think of objections or rejoinders to them.
5 Put your responses as convincingly as possible to the individual(s) concerned.
6 If they still don't agree with you, list their new objections as in (3) above. Continue in this way until you have made as much headway as possible in converting them to your point of view.

The contents and results of this exercise can be further analysed in discussion, looking for example at why individuals hold particular views, the nature of their beliefs, or whether they are based on other views which are not being clearly stated. Additionally, the exercise can be approached from a 'social skills' standpoint by installing observers and obtaining feedback from them on the effectiveness of the performance, using ratings and other kinds of comments as in previous exercises. If individuals have difficulty in choosing points of view to argue for, they could be provided with a list like the one shown opposite.

□ This basic exercise can be extended, and individuals' persuasive powers more fully explored, by conducting one or more alternative exercises like the following:

1 Individuals are asked to persuade someone of a point of view *other than* the one they hold. For example, in a group of three people, A tries to persuade B of C's point of view even though he/she disagrees with it him/herself. C acts as observer and comments afterwards.

Points of view
— Most people who are unemployed don't want to work.
— West Indians have as much right to be in this country as whites.
— Capital punishment should be brought back.
— The proper place for women is in the home.
— Anyone can become a millionaire.
— Public schools should be abolished.
— All schools should be abolished.
— Private medicine gives individuals much greater freedom of choice in treatment.
— The age of majority should be reduced to sixteen.
— Sometimes, violence is justified.
— Strikers should not be paid social security.
— Britain should give an example to the world by getting rid of its nuclear weapons.
— Standards of care in children's homes are about as good as they can be under present circumstances.

---

2 Individuals try to persuade someone else either

   (a) to agree to a point of view with which they themselves fundamentally or strongly disagree; or
   (b) to endorse a point of view that is (if possible) the actual *opposite* of their own.

3 Individuals try to persuade others of views

   (a) they used to hold, but hold no longer; or
   (b) they would like to hold, but for some reason cannot; or
   (c) they hold now, but are not sure why.

A follow-up discussion of these exercises might focus individuals' attention on such questions as: Is it easier to argue for a point of view you earnestly believe in, or for a point of view from which you feel quite detached? When persuading someone of a view other than your own, do you temporarily become convinced of it? How do people make up their minds on topics like the above? What evidence (if any) do they use? In relation to social problems or to individuals whom group members have dealt with, how are their beliefs related to their backgrounds? And how will this influence the kinds of advice they are liable to seek/accept when trying to solve their problems? Finally, all of these exercises and discussion points can be narrowed in focus to concentrate directly on difficulties which arise in counselling, based on the experience of members of the group.

All of the foregoing exercises can also be used to look at the complementary skill of resisting persuasion and influence. Those who are the targets of other people's persuasive efforts can scrutinize themselves and their responses to the experience, looking at how they felt being on the defensive; which techniques they did or didn't use to counter pressure; how successful they were at putting points to their adversaries that would raise doubts in their minds; and so on.

CHANGING THE SUBJECT

Another kind of influence which counsellors may occasionally have to exert in conversations with others is that of controlling, within broad limits, the content of the conversation in order to make it as useful and constructive as possible. Although it frequently happens that the best approach to some individual or some problem is to allow him or her to 'ventilate' or talk completely freely about something, in other instances this can serve little purpose and may actually be a barrier to problem solution. Thus counsellors may sometimes have to

— stop people in their tracks
— redirect their attention to factors they are ignoring
— get a conversation back to a topic that has been lost.

□□ This exercise is similar to the one on 'changing the tone' described earlier, but here the focus is on the verbal content of conversations rather than on their emotional significance. Individuals work in pairs, and can perhaps be 'primed' by a third person who knows the purpose of the exercise and who will act as observer. One individual is given a topic to speak to the other about and is asked to try to stick to it as much as possible. The other, who is assigned the role of 'counsellor', must try to induce the speaker to talk about something quite different. The observer notes how skilful the counsellor is in bringing his/her topic to the fore and at defeating attempts by the speaker to dwell on his/her topic. Discussion can be addressed to the tactics whereby individuals can be influenced to remain on a particular item of conversation or to switch to another if necessary.

CONFRONTATION

The most abrupt kind of influence which a helper may have to exert during a counselling session is that of confrontation. When the giving of support or advice, the expression of empathy, the use of questions, and all other devices have failed or just seem inappropriate, an absolute clash between the helper and the person with the problem may be the only conceivable way forward. We do not wish to advocate this as a regular counselling technique, but once it has been recognized that it may sometimes be necessary, then it is also worthwhile having it 'in reserve' as a counselling skill.

It is difficult to define very clearly the parameters of confrontation as a skill. Given that it is only likely to be used *in extremis*, every individual instance of a situation in which it is needed will obviously be unique. Often confrontation may be more a question of courage than of skill. Nevertheless, situations in which it may be an advisable course of action can be rehearsed using the same basic format as that employed in previous role-play exercises.

☐☐ Two group members can be asked to play counsellor and 'client' respectively, with the rest of the group observing. The clients are given overall briefs like those in the left-hand column below (which they can elaborate for themselves

'Client'	'Counsellor'
You express strong aggression either as a general attitude, or directed against a specific individual or group.	You express strong disapproval of the individual's violent attitudes and intentions.
You express vehement racist beliefs.	You must make clear your complete disavowal of racism.
You are an arrogant husband who expresses the firm belief that he has always been good to his wife.	The individual expresses views about the way he treats his wife which are completely at odds with the facts. You must put the truth to him.
You are being divorced by your husband and are fighting for the custody of your child. You earnestly believe you can look after the child better than he can. You argue this case strongly to the probation officer/social worker.	This woman is being divorced by her husband; she is fighting for custody of their only child but she has been very neglectful of it in the past when the husband was in the navy. You have to tell her that her chances of custody are less than certain.
You believe you have a very good chance of a job as a newspaper reporter that you've seen advertised. You express your confidence and enthusiasm.	This young boy or girl has completely – and persistently – unrealistic aspirations as regards work. You have to somehow bring him/her down to earth.

either by thinking about a real person whom they know or by just inventing details). The counsellor's task is to respond using confrontation, along the lines suggested in the right-hand column. Confrontation need not be accomplished rudely, or in a way which totally destroys a person's self-image or his/her relationship with a helper. Observers should pay particular attention to the extent to which the counsellors in these role-plays confront their clients with views that are unpalatable to them, but do so in a way which succeeds in keeping other aspects of their working relationship intact. Comments along these lines should be fed back to counsellors and discussed.

REWARDS AND REINFORCEMENT

Confrontation, although intended to be constructive in its effects, might be looked upon as part of the negative side of counselling; placing in the centre of an individual's vision facts or views which he or she would prefer not to perceive. The need to respond positively to an individual is much more common in most counselling activities. Yet some helpers approach the business of counselling in a cold, deadpan, or cynical frame of mind: an attitude that is likely to have the status of a self-fulfilling prophecy in its effects on people with problems. The expression of warmth, essential to effective counselling, depends in part on the adoption of a 'rewarding' approach by those who are trying to help others.

☐☐ Engaging in two- or three-person role-plays as in the preceding exercise, individuals can assess and improve their abilities in this area using the observation-feedback-practice cycle. The helpers in such role-plays should be observed with an accent being placed on the degree to which they are rewarding or reinforcing to the person they are trying to help. For this purpose the observers should look for the following kinds of behaviour:

1 *Paying attention.* The most fundamental kind of reward you can give a person is just showing you are interested in what he/she has to say.
2 *Reflecting.* As suggested previously, conveying to someone that you understand and endorse his/her feelings is a key counselling skill and is an ingredient of 'reward'.
3 *Use of reinforcers.* Observers should record the frequency and appropriateness of nods, smiles, use of the word 'yes', and other verbal and non-verbal components of social reward.
4 *Emphasis on positive statements.* By extracting and focusing on the positive elements in what someone has said; mentioning his/her good qualities; referring to the advantages of a particular situation or course of action, etc., helpers can build up positive self-attitudes in those whose views of themselves may initially be somewhat limited or deprecating.

None of this is intended to suggest that helpers should lavish unwarranted praise on their clients, should ingratiate themselves with them, or should recklessly try to inflate individuals' egos to the detriment of all other considerations. The question here, as with other constituents of counselling skill, is one of balance and aptness of response. Those who feel they put people off by failing to take advantage of opportunities to reward them should be able to benefit from the comments of observers on their behaviour, for example by having moments when they could or should have been reinforcing in a role-play pointed out to them afterwards.

Individuality in counselling

The aim of all of the exercises that have been outlined in this chapter so far has been to assist those who wish to improve their helping skills secure a more accurate impression of their strengths and weaknesses in this area, and use this information to acquire or develop their skills in ways they believe to be necessary. The aim has not, however, been to imply that there is any single correct way to go about counselling. Few prescriptions can be made about a process as complex and subtle; especially when the substance with which it deals – people's problems – is so variegated and unpredictable. Nor has the aim been to impose a uniformity of response upon those who try to help other people with their difficulties. The emphasis has been on self-discovery and on making improvements as individuals see fit – an approach which is well worth transferring to the activity of helping itself. The exercises in this section are designed to help counsellors recognize their own individual manner of dealing with people of particular kinds, and to build, if they think it necessary and desirable, greater flexibility into the way in which they react to typical statements about personal problems.

☐☐ Exploring counsellor 'styles'

The notion of counselling 'style' can be helpful here. It refers to the fact that when we meet strangers in a helping context our reactions to them (to what they say about themselves or their problems) reflect something about our own psychological make-up. Allowing for variations of several kinds – how busy we are, how well we know someone, whether or not there are others present – we tend to respond to requests for help in a broadly similar way.

The purpose of this exercise is to enable individuals to take a preliminary look at their own likely reactions when faced with problems of various kinds.

Participants in the exercise are asked to imagine they are in the midst of a first counselling session with someone. The 'client' makes a statement describing his/her problems or declaring an intention of some kind. Those taking part in the exercise must then write down (or otherwise record) what they think would be their immediate verbal response to the person whom they are counselling. They are not asked to write general notes or 'treatment plans' but instantaneous replies, using the words they would use in practice.

Leaving institutions
People about to leave prisons, borstals, children's homes, or hospital describe their plans to the counsellor.

1 An ambitious, domineering person who expresses ruthlessness towards anyone who gets in his/her way.
2 A child who refuses to go home, insisting that his/her parents hate him/her, and vice versa.
3 Someone leaving borstal who says he intends to revenge himself on the people who got him into trouble.
4 A patient leaving psychiatric hospital has completely confused and hazy aims; she does not even know where she will stay.
5 Someone, previously treated for alcoholism, who says his/her intentions after leaving are 'to have a really good drink'.
6 An individual who has no immediate family and has been suffering from depression expresses fears about being lonely after leaving.

Possible prompt
'The first thing I'm going to do when I get out of here is go round to see the kid who grassed me up and put his head through the wall. I've been in here two lousy years because of him and I'm going to get my own back.'

Possible prompt
'I just don't know what to say to my daughter any more. She's only fourteen, but she does what she likes, goes out and in when she likes, and is defiant every time I try to talk to her about it. She's completely out of control and I'm afraid she's going to get into some terrible trouble.'

Family problems
People with home difficulties of various kinds seek help.

1 An adolescent who feels that he/she is the family scapegoat threatens to run away.
2 A middle-aged wife whose children have grown up asks for help with her marriage which has 'gone dead'.
3 A young man who is becoming a burden to his elderly parents, but has no close friends or motivation to live on his own, asks why he should leave home.
4 A fraught housewife asks for help in controlling her teenage son/daughter.
5 A girl who has become pregnant and does not want her parents to know asks for advice about abortion.

The 'cases' with which participants are presented can be made up by other group members (different people might take turns to be the 'client' each time). Five or six different problems will probably be sufficient. Two sets of possible 'problems' or 'problem people' are suggested opposite; in each case one has been extracted and enlarged into the kind of statement which the individual might make. Parallel series of problems like these could be developed for many other themes − careers problems; psychiatric problems; adolescent difficulties; marital conflict; and many more.

When participants have listened to each of the problems and have recorded their responses, they are then invited to 'classify' their statements in terms of the categories shown below. A reply may of course contain a mixture of response types, for example someone may express support and then suggest a solution to a problem; in this case each part of it should be counted separately. Participants should make totals for the number of responses they have made which fall under the various headings shown.

Reflective − a non-committal type of response, usually consisting of a paraphrase of the individual's words, or some other reaction which merely shows that the counsellor is listening and gives the speaker a cue to carry on.

Evaluative − reacting in a markedly positive or negative way to what someone has said; expressing approval or disapproval; praising or rebuking; siding with or against the individual.

Supportive − an expression of sympathy with, understanding of, or support for the speaker; conveying warmth or giving encouragement.

Solution oriented − a reply which contains as its main element a positive, concrete suggestion as to a course of action the individual might take concerning his/her problem (even if this means referral to some other source of help).

Confrontation − responding to the speaker in a direct and forceful manner in order to make him/her face up to, or at least think about, something which he/she does not realize, or has been avoiding or refusing to acknowledge − with the hope of inducing change.

Clarificatory − a kind of response which asks the individual a question or invites him/her to elaborate on what has been said. This can be subdivided into two different sorts of questions:

1 *Fact-finding* – asking for another piece of information which will clarify what the individual has said, but which invites a 'closed' answer – for example by asking about previous jobs, background, age of children, or for some other item to build up a picture of the person who is speaking.

2 *Probing* – asking questions which, rather than having a ready-made answer, might induce the individual to develop a specific line of thought, explore further aspects of what he/she has said, or expand on his/her views, plans, expectations, feelings, etc.

When individuals have completed this part of the exercise, their responses can be compared and discussed. Two specific points of comparison might be, first, variations in individuals' distribution of scores amongst the various response categories (while some people will use one type of response predominantly, others will have a spread across all the types); and, second, the actual replies made by different group members to the problems with which they were presented. The former kind of feedback helps individuals gain further insight into their own particular counselling approach; the latter enables them to appreciate the diverse ways in which a single problem can be handled. A discussion on this second point can be used to lead into the next exercise which gives participants practice in responding to problems in a more flexible manner should they wish to develop their skills in this respect.

☐ Flexibility in counselling

This exercise is essentially similar to the previous one but in this case respondents are 'forced' to deal with the problems with which they are presented in a particular way or variety of ways.

A series of 'cases' or problem individuals should first be devised, of a kind parallel to those used above, and on a general area of difficulties with which individuals will have to deal in their work. The format is the same in that counsellors are presented with these problems (with one group member playing the problem people) and are asked to write down what they would say were this a 'real' counselling session. This time, however, they are either (a) told which *kind* of reply to make with each case in turn, or (b) asked to make one possible response of *every* type to each case with which they are presented.

A blank recording sheet like the one shown in the box could be used for this purpose. Again, when the exercise has been completed, comparisons should be made between the responses made by participants, looking at how easy or difficult they found this in each case, and at the actual replies they produced. The pros and cons of reacting to people's problems in various ways should then be discussed for as long as group members find it useful to do so.

Counselling responses − recording sheet

Reflective

Supportive

Evaluative

Solution oriented

Confrontation

Clarificatory − fact-finding

Clarificatory − probing

Handling problems in counselling

By this stage, if you have extensively practised the skills dealt with in preceding sections, you should, as a counsellor in training, be feeling reasonably confident about the process of counselling overall and should be capable of coping with some more difficult types of encounter. For some of the people and situations you will come across as counsellors will really put these skills to the test; some will threaten to undermine the entire process of helping itself. The exercises in this section are about some of the problems that might arise during counselling, which put any progress previously made with an individual at risk, and which may even be personally threatening to the counsellor him- or herself.

□□ There are two kinds of situation to be dealt with in this exercise:

1 *Conflict pairs.* The counsellor has to deal with two people at once; and is supposedly there to help one of the people involved — but the other keeps frustrating this in various ways.
2 *Difficult people.* Some people whom we have to help are just very awkward and burdensome to deal with, and may exhibit flippancy, inattentiveness, or hostility in varying proportions. (Some 'helpers' of course deserve to be treated in this way.) Are there better ways of handling such clients as these?

The objectives of both of these kinds of exercise is to use role-play to assess how well a situation is handled by the 'counsellor' in each case; to explore some strategies which are likely to pay off and others which aren't; to identify any skills that still need to be improved; and to evaluate whether individuals feel more able to deal with sticky situations as a result of having tried them out in practice.

□ **'Conflict pairs'**
Two group members are asked to play the following parts to put a third group member (acting as counsellor) under pressure:

1 A child and a parent who has strong ambitions for him/her, which set too high a standard for the child and are causing a lot of unhappiness.
2 Two adolescents; one who dominates the other, answers questions for him/her, and influences him/her for the worse.
3 Two adults who are locked in a relationship which is very damaging to one of them and which he/she would be better without.
4 A married couple; the wife is very afraid of her husband, has been a victim of his violence, but will not say so to the counsellor.
5 An individual in need of help and another worker who keeps getting in the way of the help the counsellor is trying to give.
6 A child and an over-protective, smothering parent, who is squashing the child's every manifestation of independence.
7 A husband and wife who take quite different views of child-rearing. One indulges the children too much and the other has to deal with the consequences, and is becoming depressed from the resultant strain.
8 The parent of a quite aggressive teenager who is going through a period of considerable instability; and the teenager who accuses the parent (unjustly) of being unfair to him/her.

9 A young couple who are in conflict over a pregnancy or abortion. The counsellor must either find a compromise *or* support the one whom he/she believes is correct and persuade the other to the same point of view.

A sample of two or three of these situations could be role-played for between five and ten minutes each, with a different group member acting as 'counsellor' in each, and his/her approach to the 'conflict' being subsequently evaluated and discussed by the whole group.

☐ **'Difficult people'**
This exercise incorporates only a slight variation on the previous one. Below are a number of 'prompts' designed for use in a series of role-plays in which counsellors are asked to imagine that they must cope with particularly difficult meetings. The group members who are given the prompts should be encouraged to take on their roles as fully and actively as possible, to make life as uneasy as they can for the trainees playing the part of the helper.

To use these prompts, a 'fish bowl' format could be set up, in which the counsellor and client are in the centre of the room, and the remaining members of the group, who will act as observers, form a rough circle around the central duo (similar to the layout shown in the photograph on p. 60). The video camera, if there is one, should be slightly farther away and should face the person role-playing the counsellor.

Like the 'conflict pair' scenes, these role-plays should be run for a maximum of ten minutes unless there is some very compelling reason for continuing longer than this. Discussion (and perhaps re-enactment of role-plays with variations of strategy) should then continue for as long as seems profitable in each case; with the circumstances, events, and characters of each encounter being related as far as possible to similar ones in group members' real work experiences.

Unless particular group members have a specific talent for portraying characters of specific types, the fairest way of allocating the 'prompts' shown here is probably just to write them on pieces of paper and draw them out of a hat. Would-be 'counsellors' could also draw lots for the order in which they will have a go at dealing with the problematic 'cases'.

☐ **Case 1**
You are feeling pretty fed up. You've 'been through the mill' of psychologists, psychiatrists, social workers, and probation officers, and as far as you're concerned they all seem much the same – not a single one has ever really tried to find out what *you* think about *your own* problems. This person you're faced with now started well; you thought he was all right for a bit, but more recently you've changed your mind since you just seem to be going through the same old routine again. He's just like all the rest. You tell him so in no uncertain terms.

☐ Case 2

You feel hopeless. You've thought and thought about your problems so much and for so long, and looked at them from every angle, but nothing seems to make you feel any better. None of the ideas that this counsellor comes up with seem to take you anywhere. You don't think it's her fault; it's just that the difficulties you're facing are so immense. You think that everything's completely hopeless; you feel absolutely despondent; and you tell the counsellor just how helpless you feel.

☐ Case 3

As far as you're concerned, everything would be all right in your marriage if it weren't for your wife's (or husband's) mother. All the things that are wrong; all the problems that come up; all the complaints your wife makes, are traceable to her influence, and quite a lot of the time to things she says to your wife about you. You haven't put a foot wrong in this marriage; it's hard to convince people of this but it really is all their fault. You suspect the counsellor imagines that you must be to blame somehow for the state of your marriage, so you decide to put his mind straight on the issue.

☐ Case 4

You agree that you've got problems − no job, hardly any money, a baby on the way, a pretty hopeless domestic arrangement, and the police after you − but as you see things there's no point in worrying about it all, what's going to happen will happen, and you'll get by somehow. This worker keeps trying to get you to *do* things about your problems, but what do they expect? There's nothing much you can do and you don't feel all that bothered about things anyway. If you listened to the worker's advice you'd never have a minute to relax. You need to make it clear that you just don't worry about things.

☐ Case 5

You find it hard to take these sorts of do-gooders seriously, and you make a joke out of everything they say. You feel quite flippant about all the kinds of things they want you to think about. The whole thing, as far as you're concerned, is just one big laugh; they can't help you and they know it. They deserve to be made fun of.

☐ Case 6

Your girl-friend, with whom you've been living, seems to be developing a relation-ship with someone else − though she's not actually said as much to you. Right now she is round at his house and you feel like going there and confronting them and bringing the whole thing out into the open. You're more angry at the way she's been treating you than jealous of the other man. Still you realize that if you do go round there things may end up in a fight. This worker thinks it's a bad idea for you to go but the more you think about it the more convinced you become that it's the best thing to do.

☐ **Case 7**

You left school about a year ago with a few O-levels, but so far you haven't managed to find a job. You're feeling a bit fed up with the prospects in your area and you'd like to move to another part of the country where your chances might be better − though you don't have any money saved. What you'd really like is a job in television. Although you haven't got any science O-levels you think you could get started as some kind of assistant and work your way up to being a producer. You tell your careers officer what your plans are to see if he/she can give you some help or suggest any openings.

☐ **Case 8**

You've been trying to see your social worker for ages but every time you ring or look in at his/her office you find that he/she is not there. You're feeling very irritated by this and now, even after you have managed to catch the worker, he/she doesn't seem very interested in your problems and has already answered the telephone once while supposedly talking to you. You ask bluntly if there is any point in continuing − if he/she is really interested in helping you.

To run these role-plays properly, those playing the part of counsellor must be given some preliminary information about the persons whom they will be facing. Some very simple vignettes could therefore be given to them along the following lines:

1 A person who was very difficult to get started with owing to his/her very cynical views of your role. Recently, however, you thought things had been progressing rather well.
2 A very negative, defeatist sort of person who won't lift a finger to help him/herself.
3 A very self-centred husband or wife whose marriage is in considerable disarray but who will not accept any of the responsibility for it.
4 A completely unmotivated, very easy-going person whose passivity − not to say sheer laziness − has got him/her into an appalling mess.
5 A fairly flippant, sometimes quite scathing person who often makes you feel uncomfortable but who has got quite serious problems.
6 An impetuous sort of person who is inclined to act first and think later − which is the reason why he/she is in difficulty now.
7 A young person not long out of school, unemployed for nearly a year, who unfortunately has a quite inaccurate estimate of his/her own abilities and prospects of employment.
8 Someone who's been trying to get in touch with you for a couple of weeks when you have been tied up elsewhere. On one occasion you were on a course, on another out on a visit, on another at a union meeting. You expect he/she will need a bit of placating because of this.

Finally, as before, the performance of the counsellors in each role-play should be reviewed and discussed, and key points about better and poorer ways to approach these situations brought out as fully as possible.

☐ Generating problems

As an alternative to the ready-prepared format for the exercises just outlined, group members may be given the opportunity to devise 'difficult cases' for each other. The group is divided into two smaller groups, and each must develop a set of perhaps five 'problem people'; these are then role-played for members of the other group who have to act as counsellors. This exercise also provides an opportunity for group members to rehearse various possibilities for dealing with real individuals whom they have in mind.

☐ Critical incidents

A final exercise that could be mounted as an aid to coping with particularly difficult situations is the reconstruction by individuals of one encounter in which they were involved (or which happened to one of their number) in which a counselling session went markedly astray or became pointless, harrowing, or even destructive. This exercise is essentially the same as that suggested in Chapter 2 but here the incident is re-enacted so that the participants can explore what occurred in more depth, assemble some alternative ways of managing it, and practise them in further role-plays.

Self-monitoring of skills development

It is unlikely that those learning to become helpers will wish to undertake every exercise that has been included in this chapter. People may be already fairly well equipped with some skills; may regard some others as less important for their work; and may concentrate on only a few areas in which they are not quite sure of themselves or in which they feel that their skills need improvement. There is nothing definitive about the types of skill and the specific series of exercises presented in this book. If you are involved in this kind of training, however, you will certainly find it useful to keep some kind of record of the work you are doing and the progress you are making – even if that is only to say that you have tried an exercise over and over again but do not feel you can make much headway in that particular sphere.

A record of this kind could be cast in a variety of forms. One might be an open-ended diary in which you list various exercises in which you and/or your group have been involved together with your comments on them. Another might be a summary sheet in which you map out changes in ratings you have had from other group members over a series of role-plays on one particular skill. Yet another might be a self-monitoring 'log' in which you list the skills you want to develop, the exercises you have undertaken, the results in each case, and the subsequent outcomes when you attempted to deploy these skills in real counselling situations. One format for maintaining such a record might look like this:

'Skills	Training exercises	No. of sessions	Results	Tried in practice?

This format can be varied to include whichever kinds of information seem most appropriate to you to remember. There could also be space for the comments of others − your fellow students, colleagues at work, clients themselves, and friends. In this way you will gain as comprehensive a picture as possible of yourself as a helper and as accurate an impression as possible of the effects your work is having on others; possibly the most valuable kind of information anyone involved in such an activity could wish to have.

Notes and references

COUNSELLING IN GENERAL

The starting point for most contemporary approaches to counselling is the work of Carl Rogers; see *On Becoming a Person* (Boston: Houghton Mifflin, 1961) and *Client-Centred Therapy* (Boston: Houghton Mifflin, 1951). More recent developments of Rogers's ideas are represented in the work of Carkhuff and Truax; see R. R. Carkhuff (1969) *Helping and Human Relations* vols 1 and 2 (New York: Holt, Rinehart, and Winston); and C. B. Truax and R. R. Carkhuff (1967) *Toward Effective Counselling and Psychotherapy* (Chicago: Aldine).

BEHAVIOURAL COUNSELLING

An outline of recent developments in behavioural approaches to counselling can be found in J. D. Krumboltz and C. E. Thoresen (eds) (1976) *Counselling Methods*

(New York: Holt, Rinehart, and Winston). This book contains case studies of the application of behavioural techniques. See also A. E. Ivey and L. Simek-Downing (1980) *Counselling and Psychotherapy: Skills, Theories, and Practice* (Englewood Cliffs, N.J.: Prentice-Hall).

THE SKILLS APPROACH

Skills-based approaches to counselling are developed and applied in A. E. Ivey and J. Authier (1978) *Microcounselling* (Springfield, Ill.: Charles C. Thomas); G. Egan (1981) *The Skilled Helper* (Monterey, Cal.: Brooks-Cole); E. A. Munro, R. J. Manthei, and J. J. Small (1979) *Counselling: A Skills Approach* (Wellington: Methuen (New Zealand)); and O. Hargie, C. Saunders, and D. Dickson (1981) *Social Skills in Interpersonal Communication* (London: Croom Helm).

RESEARCH ON EFFECTIVE HELPERS

The concepts of genuineness, empathy, and respect are derived from the work of Carl Rogers (1957) The Necessary and Sufficient Conditions of Therapeutic Personality Change, *Journal of Consulting Psychology* 21: 95–103.

See also: M. Yelloly (1972) The Helping Relationship, in D. Jehu, P. Hardiker, M. Yelloly, and M. Shaw (eds) *Behaviour Modification in Social Work* (Chichester: Wiley); the book by Truax and Carkhuff cited above; or D. A. Kolb and R. E. Boyatzis (1974) On the Dynamics of the Helping Relationship, a chapter in D. A. Kolb, I. M. Rubin, and J. M. McIntyre (eds), *Organisational Psychology: A Book of Readings* (Englewood Cliffs, N.J.: Prentice-Hall). For recent reviews of research in this area, see the chapters Research on Therapist Variables in Relation to Process and Outcome (by M. B. Parloff, I. E. Waskow, and B. E. Wolfe); The Relation of Process to Outcome in Psychotherapy (by D. E. Orlinsky and K. I. Howard); and Research on the Teaching and Learning of Psychotherapeutic Skills (by R. G. Matarazzo); in S. L. Garfield and A. E. Bergin (eds) (1978) *Handbook of Psychotherapy and Behaviour Change* (New York: Wiley). These chapters are concerned principally with therapy as such, but outlines of research on counselling can be found within them. Finally, see B. Hugman (1977) *Act Natural* (London: Bedford Square Press).

FIELDS OF APPLICATION

For discussion of some of the issues at stake in areas of work in which counselling is used, see the following:
On social work: B. Jordan (1979) *Helping in Social Work* (London: Routledge).
On schools counselling: D. Hamblin (1974) *The Teacher and Counselling* (Oxford: Blackwell).

On careers counselling: B. Hopson and J. Hayes (1968) *The Theory and Practice of Vocational Guidance* (Oxford: Pergamon).

On marriage guidance counselling: J. Dominian (1968) *Marital Breakdown* (Harmondsworth: Penguin).

On death counselling: E. Kubler-Ross (1969) *On Death and Dying* (London: Tavistock).

For a useful review of a wide range of methods that can be used within counselling, see F. H. Kanfer and A. P. Goldstein (eds) (1980) *Helping People Change: A Textbook of Methods* (Oxford: Pergamon).

SKILLS EXERCISES

For background information or further ideas concerning the exercises described in this chapter, readers should consult:

For the distinction between attending and influencing skills: A. E. Ivey and J. Authier (1978) *Microcounselling* (Springfield, Ill.: Charles C. Thomas).

On skill ratings: A. P. Goldstein, R. P. Sprafkin, and N. J. Gershaw (1976) *Skill Training for Community Living* (New York: Pergamon Press).

On role-reversal: F. M. Culbertson (1957) Modification of An Emotionally Held Attitude through Role Playing. *Journal of Abnormal and Social Psychology* **54**: 230–33.

Listening and following: see the book by Ivey and Authier already cited; and P. Trower, B. Bryant, and M. Argyle (1978) *Social Skills and Mental Health* (London: Methuen).

On questioning and types of questions: O. Hargie, C. Saunders, and D. Dickson (1981) *Social Skills in Interpersonal Communication* (London: Croom Helm); and E. A. Munro, R. J. Manthei, and J. J. Small (1979) *Counselling: A Skills Approach* (Wellington: Methuen (New Zealand).

For exercises on information giving and teaching in general: G. Brown (1975) *Microteaching* (London: Methuen), and (1979) *Lecturing and Explaining* (London: Methuen). For an insightful and amusing treatment of official attempts to give information see T. Vernon (1980) *Gobbledegook: A Critical Review of Official Forms and Leaflets – and How to Improve Them* (London: National Consumer Council).

For a consideration of press releases and other aspects of relations with the media see D. MacShane (1979) *Using the Media* (London: Pluto Press).

On the skill of reflection: see the books by Ivey and Authier, and by Hargie, Saunders, and Dickson, mentioned above, and also: M. R. Uhlemann, G. W. Lea, and G. L. Stone (1976) Effect of Instructions and Modelling on Trainees Low in Interpersonal-Communication Skills. *Journal of Counselling Psychology* **23**: 509–13.

On the perception and communication of feelings, and on 'non-verbal communication' in general: M. Argyle (1975) *Bodily Communication* (London: Methuen); M. L. Knapp (1980) *Essentials of Nonverbal Communication* (New York: Holt, Rinehart, and Winston); and M. Argyle, F. Alkema, and R. Gilmour (1972) The Communication of

Friendly and Hostile Attitudes by Verbal and Non-Verbal Signals. *European Journal of Social Psychology* **1**: 385–402.

On self-disclosure: see S. Jourard (1964) *The Transparent Self* (New York: Van Nostrand), and (1971) *Self-disclosure* (New York: Wiley); G. L. Stone and I. Gotlib (1975) Effect of Instructions and Modelling on Self-Disclosure. *Journal of Counselling Psychology* **22**: 288–93; and D. McGuire, M. H. Thelen, and T. Amolsch (1975) Interview Self-Disclosure as a Function of Length of Modelling and Descriptive Instructions. *Journal of Consulting and Clinical Psychology* **43**: 356–62.

On the importance of empathy and on empathy training: see R. R. Carkhuff (1969) *Helping and Human Relations* (New York: Holt, Rinehart, and Winston); S. J. Frank (1978) Just Imagine How I Feel: How to Improve Empathy Through Training in Imagination, in J. L. Singer and K. S. Pope (eds) *The Power of Human Imagination: New Methods in Psychotherapy* (New York: Plenum Press); and S. G. Toukmanian and D. L. Rennie (1975) Microcounselling versus Human Relations Training: Relative Effectiveness with Undergraduate Trainees. *Journal of Counselling Psychology* **22**: 345–52.

On rewards and reinforcement: see W. S. Verplanck (1955) The Control of the Content of Conversation: Reinforcement of Statements of Opinion. *Journal of Abnormal and Social Psychology* **51**: 668–76; and J. M. Rogers (1960) Operant Conditioning in a Quasi-Therapy Setting. *Journal of Abnormal and Social Psychology* **60**: 247–52.

Finally, for a useful set of readings on different aspects of counselling, see A. W. Bolger (ed.) (1982) *Counselling in Britain: A Reader* (London: Batsford); and, for a wide-ranging textbook on the field of counselling as a whole, consult R. Nelson-Jones (1982) *The Theory and Practice of Counselling Psychology* (Eastbourne: Holt, Rinehart, and Winston).

5 Group leading

It is not unusual for even quite skilled and experienced helpers to disclaim any interest in working with people in groups. They do so for a variety of reasons. One is that despite the wide currency of the idea and the existence of a vast literature on the subject, it is still not clear to a good many people what it is that groups *do* or *why* they are supposed to be such a good thing. Part of the blame for this lack of understanding must be laid at the door of those practitioners and theorists who envelop their work in a veritable smoke-screen of wordy obfuscation (Bion 1970). An allied difficulty stems from the glimpses of such groups in action which can be gleaned from their writings: prolonged silences, emotional outbursts, displays of 'therapeutic' anger, 'hot seats', and the like; all accompanied by warnings to the uninitiated to 'keep out'. Seen in those terms, groups seem so remote from the work that many helpers do with individuals, and so full of dangers and difficulties, that they are pleased to heed the warnings and do other things instead.

But the groups which are written about in this way are very unrepresentative. Most of human life revolves around the membership of collective entities that extend from informal gatherings to complicated bureaucratic structures. The groups organized by helpers constitute only a tiny, and not all that typical part of this wide spectrum. Even less typical are those training or 'sensitivity' groups which take as their topic the internal mechanics and dynamics of the groups themselves − a device which appears to baffle or infuriate as many people as it helps; hence the 'danger' signs with which their devotees surround them (Rice 1965).

Straightforward group discussion, on the other hand, is more or less an extension of the everyday experience of most people and is a method that can be used with safety and confidence by perfectly ordinary helpers. Discussion of this sort can be thought of as a 'multi-channel interview' and can be tackled in basically the same way as individual counselling sessions.

It requires preparation; defining aims, recruiting members, and starting off the discussion; and some ideas for keeping it going, coping with any problems that crop up, and summarizing the proceedings at the end. These are the tasks of the group leader, and they can be performed better or worse, but it is worth remembering that some of the most effective groups operate on a self-help basis; that is in the entire absence of trained or qualified group leaders of any description.

Why groups?

If you are going to run a group for people who have some kind of personal problem it is a good idea to begin by being clear in your own mind about what they – and you – might get from the experience. Just getting together for a gossip, although it may be good fun, is not sufficient reason for arranging a group. Try identifying a set of individuals you might wish to help in this way, and make a statement of the aims that group meetings with them might pursue.

If you were working with the parents of *spina bifida* children, for example, the aims of a group meeting might be:

1 To inform them more fully about medical knowledge concerning the condition of *spina bifida*.
2 To swap experiences of coping with the difficulties of a handicapped child.
3 To provide mutual support.

Given these aims, a typical group meeting might consist of an initial coffee-and-biscuits session as parents arrived, a brief talk by a medical person followed by questions, and a chaired discussion on a pre-arranged topic, plus 'any other business' when members raised their own concerns.

If you were working with unemployed young people, the aims of a group might be:

1 To give encouragement and support.
2 To share job search experiences and set-backs.
3 To organize leisure and other activities.

If you were running a staff-development group in a residential work setting, the aims might be:

1 To let off some of the steam generated by the pressures of daily life in a residential setting.
2 To discuss difficult cases and how to handle them.
3 To identify staff training needs.

☐ Make a list of *four* groups that you could run with the people you help and v
a set of aims for each of them. This might entail only one main aim per group, or
several.

☐ Repeat the exercise; this time identifying aims for *two* staff training or development groups at your (intended) place of work.

Fifteen good reasons for running groups

Because of their endless variety it is not possible to give an exhaustive list of good reasons
for running groups; the fifteen that follow have not been arranged in any order of priority.

1 *Expressing a point of view.* Modern family life and a system of universal education have
   between them failed to equip quite a lot of people with the confidence and skill to
   make contributions to debate and discussion. A small, purposeful, relaxed, and well-
   led group provides an opportunity for making good these deficits.

2 *Conversational skills.* An extension of self-expression is having to respond to the views
   of others and engaging in simple conversation – group discussion provides a forum
   for the development and exercise of these skills.

3 *Exchanging information.* A group can also act as an informal form of education in its
   broadest sense by promoting the exchange of information between those who take part
   in it; information about themselves, and their problems, about the local community –
   its services and facilities, and a thousand and one other matters of fact that they
   happen to know about.

4 *Sharing experiences.* Self-help groups tend to work oɴ the principle that 'a trouble
   shared is a trouble halved' and although the arithmetic may not be the same for everyone, it is certainly true that swapping experiences can be of value to individuals who
   share common problems.

5 *Grasping concepts.* Besides allowing members to talk about themselves, group discussion also appears to promote effective learning about concepts and abstractions.
   And it does so in a way that is as good as, and in some ways better than, listening to
   lectures, reading books or articles, or writing essays, thinking, and engaging in private
   study. Discussion is not of course a substitute for any of these methods, but a useful
   adjunct to them.

6 *Giving and getting feedback.* One of the most powerful learning mechanisms at work in
   groups is that of 'feedback'; the responses which members make to each other's
   contributions. Feedback may be positive or negative, or neutral, and may be directed
   both at the person *and* at what he or she has said.

7 *Learning about self.* One of the consequences of feedback, of hearing how others
   respond to the content and the manner of what you say, is that of heightened self-
   awareness, a deeper and richer knowledge of oneself. Even the effort of formulating a
   view or defending it against attack by others can be self-revelatory.

8 *Learning about others.* The opposite is also true; listening to what others have to say about a topic, responding to what they say, and taking some account of their views, is also a considerable learning experience about other people.

9 *Changing attitudes.* Exposure to the views of others, and their comments on one's own positions can hardly fail to have *some* effect on personal attitudes; if it is only to strengthen the fervour with which they are held. It more frequently happens, however, that views change in the direction of those held by the majority within a group. How desirable that is depends on the nature of the values the rest of them hold. In some instances the worker may be concerned to shift dominant values within a group in different directions; e.g. away from racist or sexist stereotypes.

10 *Learning new behaviour.* An established and relaxed group is a suitable environment in which to try out new behaviour for the first time, and to practise a variety of ways of responding to situations.

11 *Increasing self-confidence.* Although it is not always possible to pursue increased self-confidence as an explicit aim, it often turns out to be a welcome by-product of other group activities.

12 *Problem solving and decision making.* If two heads are better than one, then ten are even better. A positively motivated and well-integrated group can help individuals to resolve personal dilemmas and find solutions to seemingly insoluble problems.

13 *Discussing feelings.* Individuals often feel that they are alone in the feelings they have about themselves and their lives. Group discussion of some of these feelings usually reveals that this is not the case. A sympathetic audience may encourage some individuals to confront and acknowledge some of their innermost feelings in a positive and constructive way.

14 *Working with others.* An educational tradition which emphasizes individual excellence has masked to some extent the need to learn how to work with other people. Membership of a successful group can be an eye-opener for those who have never known the pleasure and profit that accrue from co-operation and collaboration.

15 *Mutual aid and support.* An allied product of the good group is the sense of belonging it engenders and the atmosphere of mutual aid that permeates its proceedings.

These good reasons for running groups are general ones that may require rewriting for specific events, and personal experience will suggest others to add to the list. It is also unlikely that any one group will enjoy all of these benefits, but it is the job of the group leader or organizer to make sure that as many members enjoy as many of them as possible, as often as possible.

☐ Think of some of the groups you currently belong to, or have belonged to in the past; these may be family groups, groups of friends, clubs, societies, formal or informal associations at work or in the community. What are some of the benefits you have enjoyed from your various memberships? Some of them may fit the categories in the list above, or they may be quite different. To what extent are these benefits reproducible in groups you could run for some of the people you are working with? What would you need to do as a group organizer to make such benefits accessible to its members?

It may be useful to do this exercise in conversation with someone else.

Recruiting groups

However good the reasons may be for running groups, and no matter how skilled and dedicated the organizer, nothing can happen without the presence and co-operation of suitable group members. In some places this is easier to arrange than in others; in schools, colleges, and residential establishments of various sorts, there are captive and semi-captive audiences for group activities. For workers in community-based agencies and organizations, potential group members are widely dispersed and not necessarily convinced of the value of joining one. Considerable effort may therefore be necessary to ensure first of all that *anyone* comes along to a group meeting, and secondly that anyone who *does* is likely to benefit from the experience.

Quantity may appear to be the lesser of these two problems, and on occasions it presents no difficulties at all to the group organizer, but unless intended members (a) know that the group is taking place, and (b) have some idea of its purposes, they are unlikely to present themselves at the inaugural meeting. In some settings, a rough rule of thumb appears to be that invitations have to be extended to twice the desired number of participants; but if the take-up rate exceeds 50 per cent the room may suddenly appear to be too small.

The question of *quality* is altogether more problematic. There are no real rules to guide the worker about the selection and composition of good groups. A randomly assembled collection of individuals can turn out to be as good as the most carefully chosen and subtly balanced selection. The exercises that follow are intended only to ensure that the aims of the group are communicated and that some thought is given to the issue of composition.

☐ Explaining the benefits

Look at the list of groups and the aims you generated for them at the beginning of this chapter. Now add some of the benefits that you would expect group members to gain from their membership and participation. Write out a simple letter to a possible participant explaining the purpose of the group and the likely benefits to the individual concerned of taking part in it.

How would you explain the benefits of group membership in any of your groups to the following individuals?

— A parent who is at risk of perpetrating violence on a child
— Someone who is very depressed
— An unemployed man aged forty-seven
— A shy and friendless teenager

☐ **Advertising**

Devise a single sheet advertisement for a group you wish to run, which you could pin on a noticeboard or a waiting room wall, and designed to appeal to, and be intelligible to, as wide a cross-section of people as you can make it.

☐ **Selling**

Ask a friend to role-play the part of a person who is reluctant to join your group and also able to articulate coherent objections to it. If your friend is truly obstinate you are unlikely to win the argument, but it is good practice for how things really happen. The exercise can be repeated using the following role-play prompts for the leader and a prospective-but-resistant group member.

Leader: You are organizing a discussion group for people with chronic back-pain problems. You think a particular sufferer would gain a lot from membership. She is a rather friendless woman in her middle years, living on her own.

Potential group member: You are a middle-aged woman suffering from chronic back-pain. You have a lot of pain but subscribe to a 'suffer in silence' philosophy. Nor are you especially sympathetic towards other sufferers. You are also quite shy and reserved and do not like revealing yourself to others. When you are asked to join a group to talk about back-pain problems you resist the idea with every argument you can think of.

☐☐ **'Ideal' member profile**

When you have decided on the aims of your group and thought about how to present them, draw up a short list of the characteristics which an 'ideal' member of your group would possess. For example a 'battered' wives group 'ideal' member might look something like this:

— Sufficiently recovered from last attack to take part.
— Interested to some extent in the problems of others in the same situation.
— Able to attend weekly group meetings.
— Motivated to do something about her position.

It is unlikely that this idealized member will ever appear in person at a group meeting, but the actual characteristics of those who do take part can be compared from time to time with this 'ideal' profile. If it is consistently wide of the real members of the target group, it may be in need of some revision.

Preparing for a group discussion

The most straightforward kinds of group are those convened to discuss concrete topics, for example smoking, ante-natal care, child-rearing problems, obesity, finding work, accommodation, sex, dealing with officials, shyness – the list can be as long as you like. Preparing for a discussion like this can be done as though for an interview or counselling session, that is by writing out a simple discussion plan. This is not meant to be a rigid formula to be followed to the letter by a group, but a source of ideas to fall back on if the conversation flags. If you were leading a discussion for some young people about sex, you might want to cover some of these topics:

Why is sex such a problem?
Attitudes – parental and peers
Changing physiology
Dating behaviour
Non-sexual relations with the opposite sex
Falling in and out of love
Finishing relationships
Overcoming shyness
Appearance
Morality
Contraception
Abortion
Venereal disease

The joys of sex
Romance
Love-making
Children
Companionship

The subject is so broad and so rich that it could go in any of a hundred different directions; the first priority of the group leader is to select some areas which group members will find most stimulating and relevant to their own concerns. Each of the headings could also make a solid subject for discussion in its own right. Under some of the headings it may help to think of some direct questions to pose to the group; for example under 'Overcoming shyness' you could ask questions like:

— Does anybody here find it difficult to talk to people you have just met?
— What do you say to someone you would like to dance with?

— What is it that makes you feel nervous when you meet someone of the opposite sex who you think is attractive or interesting?
— Do you know anyone who isn't at all shy? What sort of person is that?
— Does shyness disappear as you get older?
— Is there anything you can do to overcome shyness?
— What sorts of people make you feel really at ease and not self-conscious? How would *you* put a really shy person at ease?
— What things do you like talking about with your personal friends?

These questions, like the headings themselves, are best kept in reserve in case the discussion dies away altogether. When the members of a group have their own concerns they wish to talk about, the leader's role is limited to encouraging the less talkative and helping to draw conclusions at the end.

When a discussion fails to get off the ground at all, it is a good idea to have at least one other prepared topic up your sleeve; it may never be needed but it lends confidence to your performance to know that it is there.

☐ Take the single issue of *moral rules* as they apply to sexual conduct, for example, and make a note of some of the issues and questions you would use in discussing them.

☐ Now think of some of the groups you encounter in your helping work, and identify between five and ten topics which they would be interested in talking about. Take two of these topics and make notes on some headings for a discussion.

Ice-breakers

When a group first assembles it is normal for different members to feel degrees of unease that range from the very slight to those verging on panic at the prospect of interacting with so many strangers. In time these feelings will ease, but to begin with they may cast long shadows over the proceedings, and it has become usual to initiate a group with 'ice-breaking' exercises of various kinds. And even when all the participants are already known to each other it sometimes makes sense to employ an ice-breaker simply to signal a change in purpose and atmosphere.

You can begin by asking all those present to introduce themselves to the rest of the group:

'I'm Stella Wilkinson. I work for the local authority as a home help organizer. I've been doing that for five years, before that I was bringing up two children. I'm here to learn something that will make me a more effective organizer at work.'

Two problems with this approach: for shy people this way of starting can become a dreaded ordeal; it is not always clear what is expected of participants, and what the first person says may provide a pattern that the rest will follow willy-nilly.

To counter the first of these difficulties it may be better to start by asking participants to pair off with people they have never met before, to talk to them for five minutes or so, finding out who they are, and what they do, and why they have come. When the time has elapsed, the pairs thus formed can be asked to join another pair, to introduce themselves to the others and to spend another five minutes in mutual conversation. Alternatively each person in the pairs can be asked to introduce his or her partner to the rest of the group, which is one way round the deep shyness that affects some individuals; or the members of the fours can take turns to introduce each other.

In groups that are not too large it can be useful to ask group members to write their names on pieces of paper which they stand on the floor in front of them.

☐ **Make a list of ice-breaking exercises that you could use with different kinds of groups in your work.**

Agreeing the conditions

Amongst the reasons for the negative responses some people make to the idea of taking part in a group discussion are uncertainty about what is going to happen and what will be asked of them, and a general fearfulness about exposing themselves to the dislike or ridicule of others by their behaviour or utterances. These are natural fears that must be respected and dealt with as openly as possible by making clear to all the participants, both when recruiting and when the group begins, under what conditions they will attend. So whatever the aims of the group, the conditions which apply to its conduct might be expressed as follows:

— Attendance is voluntary – members are free to leave at any time.
— Participation is voluntary – no pressure will be put on anyone to speak or respond.
— Any personal information revealed by group members will be regarded as confidential, and not divulged to third parties without the permission of the person concerned.

If the group members are likely to be inconsiderate to each other, as in some groups of young people for example, then further 'conditions' may need to be spelled out:

1 Everyone to have the opportunity to speak and be heard.
2 One person to speak at a time.
3 No personal attacks on others.

Whatever these conditions are, they should be made very clear to all those taking part, so that they may choose whether to remain in the group or not.

In places where group discussion is not the 'normal' way of working, in schools, for example, where subject teachers take responsibility for pastoral or career counselling, or in prisons where 'discipline' staff run pre-release classes, a session devoted to conditions can also be used to signify a change of gear, a shift in roles, and different terms of reference.

☐ **Prepare and then discuss with a colleague some conditions for groups that you might run with:**

    (a) **Adolescent offenders on supervision orders**
    (b) **School refusers**
    (c) **Parents of girls with anorexia nervosa**
    (d) **Former mental hospital patients living in a hostel**

Starting a discussion

When everyone has been assembled, the aims of the group explained, the conditions of membership agreed, and personal introductions effected, it is time to start the discussion. If the members of a group are easy in each other's company and experienced in the ways of groups, it may require nothing more than an announcement of the topic to provoke immediate and animated debate. If not, a few sentences by way of introduction; raising some of the issues, pointing to some facts or opinions, and asking one or two direct questions, can be a good way to begin:

> 'We are going to talk about smoking in this group. Why do people do it? What are the effects on themselves and other people? Should the law make it more difficult for people to smoke? Is advertising of tobacco a good or a bad thing? Is it possible to give up smoking for good? I'd like to start with the reasons why people smoke.
>
> 'I think when I started, which was when I was fourteen, it was a mixture of curiosity, because my parents smoked, and of wanting to look mature and sophisticated, and because it was ever so slightly naughty. I don't think it ever entered my head that it might be unpleasant or dangerous either for myself or for other people. But it *was* extremely unpleasant to begin with and I had to persevere for quite a long time before I began to appreciate what are called the pleasures of smoking; and then I was hooked, and began smoking more and more, and found it very difficult to give up for a long time.
>
> 'Well, that's my story. How did other people start?'

That is of course only *one* way of starting a discussion on smoking; some general questions, a bit of autobiographical self-disclosure, and a specific question to the members of the group. Alternatively you could start by giving some facts and figures or reading an extract from a newspaper article.

Discussion can of course start as a natural consequence of many other sorts of activity: role-plays, watching films, going on visits, listening to speakers; but in a group where discussion is the main reason for meeting, any of these stimuli need to be kept to a minimum; no more than five minutes at the most − otherwise the nature of the occasion is changed into something else.

☐ Working in small groups of four, prepare and then practise presenting a simple introduction to a group discussion on a topic of your choice. Your 'audience' can provide feedback on how well you did, and you can provide the same service for them.

☐ If there are enough people it is possible to organize a 'knock-out' competition for group discussion starters. The contest commences in pairs where each person presents an opening statement; the pair must then agree on the winner, who goes forward to the next round, which takes place in a foursome formed by joining forces with another pair. Two presentations are made and a winner agreed who goes forward to the next round in which two groups of four participate; and so on until the champion is crowned.

Recording what goes on in groups

CONTRIBUTION RATES

As with interviews, the simplest measure that can be made of behaviour in groups is how much each member says. This can be recorded for a group on a 'wheel' chart.

Each member of the group is assigned a segment of the wheel and the observer makes a mark for each statement uttered by that person, regardless of its length or content or direction. The *number* of contributions generally correlates with the *amount* of speech contained in them, so there is no need to time them individually.

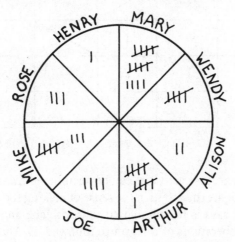

The completed wheel provides an approximate measure of the relative contributions made to discussion by the members and by the leader of a group. A single score like this may not tell you too much about your group leading skills, but a series of recordings taken over time with the same group, or whole sets relating to different groups, begin to add up to evidence that can be taken fairly seriously. If they reveal that the leader is speaking a great deal, it may be due to the nature of the group and of the topic it addresses, or it may be a sign of nervousness, or of basic style.

The record for a single group may also say something about the balance of contributions as between individual members and suggest the desirability of securing a more even spread. The problems of the 'silent' and the 'dominant' group member are looked at in more detail below (p. 140).

WHO SPEAKS TO WHOM

Just as important and interesting as the *quantity* of speech in a group is its *direction* – who speaks to whom, in other words.

This can be plotted using a matrix like this one, which records the number and direction of contributions in a six-person group, including the leader, who is male.

| | | | Receivers | | | | |
Senders	Leader	Tom	Jill	Jack	Jane	Anne	
Leader		1	1	–	5	3	10
Tom	2		2	–	1	–	5
Jill	1	1		–	3	2	7
Jack	–	–	1		–	–	1
Jane	4	1	2	–		4	11
Anne	2	–	1	–	5		8
	9	3	7	0	14	9	42

Several features of this group's activities can be deciphered from the scores in the boxes. The leader does not dominate the group in the sense of making too many interventions, but the direction of what he says is heavily biased towards Jane and Anne. Jane is clearly a central person in the deliberations of the group, followed by Anne and the group leader;

and Jane and Anne form a dominant duo in the proceedings. Jack, on the other hand, is an isolate member, speaking only once, and not spoken to by anyone else. Perhaps, with hindsight, the leader should have addressed one or two remarks in the direction of Jack to encourage his participation in the group, and maybe not have spoken quite so much to Jane.

It should be noted that this scoring matrix does not constitute a sociometry in which *preferences* are expressed by group members about each other, a procedure which can often be difficult to interpret without causing personal offence to little-preferred individuals.

ANALYSING CONTRIBUTIONS

More complex to record and interpret but equally important for understanding how a group works is the *content* of what the members say to each other. The most common categories which are used to describe contributions to group discussion are '*task oriented*', and '*group oriented*'.

Task-oriented responses are directed towards the goals of the group: reaching a decision, agreeing on something, talking about a specific topic; business-like remarks that move the agenda of the meeting on towards a concrete outcome.

Group-oriented responses by contrast relate much more to what is going on in the group and between its members, regardless of the business in hand. These may be positive or negative comments directed at one or more group members, for example paying compliments, making critical noises, cracking jokes, resolving conflicts, making people feel good – or bad.

These two types of contribution by individuals can be recorded in this way:

	Group oriented	Task oriented
John	⌗⌗⌗‍	ǀǀ
Linda	ǀǀǀ	⌗⌗⌗ ǀǀǀ
Mary	ǀǀ	ǀ

Neither type is better than the other. Indeed, both are essential to the maintenance of good group discussion. If you record and analyse the whole of the transactions that take place in a group, it may emerge that one or more individuals act to help the group get on with its tasks, whilst others help it to hang together. Good group leading permits and encourages both styles of participation in judicious proportions, related to the nature of a particular discussion.

☐☐ Slow-motion discussion

It is often difficult, if not impossible, during the cut and thrust of actual interaction in groups to keep an eye on what is happening, especially when you are in the thick of it yourself. External observers can help by watching and reporting afterwards. Video tape recordings make it possible to look at the action in a more leisurely way, stopping the tape as required, running action replays, etc., but there is a considerable loss of immediacy.

Another way of enabling individuals to look at their own behaviour as it is actually happening, is to conduct a 'slow-motion' discussion. This can be done between individuals, but it is more lively and productive when small groups are used.

Divide the participants into two equally sized groups, between four and six is best, and locate each in a separate room. Pick a subject of interest and concern to those taking part; for example a policy statement for admissions to a residential establishment; a job description for a director of social services; priorities in community planning; educational provision in a particular inner-city area and some recommendations for action; how to set up a toy library; criteria for allocating home helps; etc. One group begins by making an opening statement, limited to not more than three or four sentences, which is written down and conveyed to the other group. The receiving group discusses it and prepares a reply. Whilst they are doing this, the transmitting group considers the message they have just sent and makes some attempt to categorize it.

In a 'blind' discussion like this one there would not, of course, be many 'group' oriented contributions, but the task oriented ones can be allocated to categories in any of a number of analytic schemes currently in use. Neil Rackham, for instance, suggests that at their most basic, contributions to deliberative discussion can be classified as 'initiating', 'reacting', or 'clarifying' (Rackham and Morgan 1977). He also uses a more complex set of categories:

Helpful proposing
Unhelpful proposing

Supporting
Disagreeing

Building
Criticizing
Clarifying
Confusing
Other behaviour: appropriate
Other behaviour: inappropriate

Alternatively the well-known Bales categories (opposite) can be used (Bales 1950), although these are more complicated, or a self-made list.

Group interaction record

Member no.	1	2	3	4
Encourages				
Agrees, accepts				
Arbitrates				
Proposes action				
Asks suggestions				
Gives opinion				
Asks opinion				
Gives information				
Seeks information				
Poses problem				
Defines position				
Asks position				
Routine direction				
Depreciates self				
Autocratic				
Disagrees				
Self-assertion				
Active aggression				
Passive aggression				

When the second group has made its reply, it spends the waiting time analysing and categorizing first of all its own reply, and then the message from the other group which preceded it. A time limit, say five minutes per communication period, should be set and an overall limit on the length of time or the number of exchanges allowed; perhaps twelve messages in total, that is six each way, or an hour's discussion. At the end both groups should discuss together the fruits of the exercise and compare the categories they have awarded to each of the contributions, both their own and those of the responding group.

The exercise gives practice in the use of category systems, *and* allows the participants to decipher the structure of their debate as it happens. The fruitfulness or otherwise of the discussion may be traceable to the nature of the contributions and reactions of the two groups taking part.

Group climate

Groups can be counted successful if they achieve some of their stated aims, but they also possess an independent and more intangible dimension which is best, if not very clearly, defined as 'climate'. A group may fail to do much but still be a nice place to be. Participants are aware of this atmosphere on a continuous basis, and these subjective impressions can be made both explicit and more precise. One way of doing this is to complete simple word checks or rating scales; for example:

☐ Here are some words that describe the atmosphere in groups:

Purposeful   Apathetic   Supportive   Anxious   Co-operative   Volatile
    Welcoming   Angry   Stable   Boring   Well-organized

Underline *five* words that best describe the group you are in.

Do you think this group is:

Warm	⌊_____⌊_____⌊_____⌊_____⌋	Cold
Serious	⌊_____⌊_____⌊_____⌊_____⌋	Funny
Relaxed	⌊_____⌊_____⌊_____⌊_____⌋	Tense
Hostile	⌊_____⌊_____⌊_____⌊_____⌋	Friendly

Put a ring round the point on each scale which describes how it feels to be in the group.

These indications of group climate can be completed by all the participants, either at the end of the discussion or at intervals during it, and can be compared afterwards to determine the extent of agreement or disagreement amongst members.

A two-dimensional analysis of behaviour in groups

There are numerous ways of analysing what people do in groups. This exercise looks at two dimensions along which individual behaviour can be placed, either by self-report – the person's own perception of his or her own performance, or by other people observing and appraising the person in action in a group. The person rating or being rated can be the leader *or* a group member (Gough 1957).

☐☐ Give each person a copy of the following list of words that describe some aspects of behaviour in groups:

Acquiesces	Disapproves
Advises	Evades
Agrees	Initiates
Analyses	Judges
Assists	Leads
Concedes	Obliges
Co-operates	Relinquishes
Co-ordinates	Resists
Criticizes	Retreats
Directs	Withdraws

Ask each person to select the ten words that best describe the group behaviour of the person under scrutiny. These can then be located in the boxes below by under-lining the selected ones.

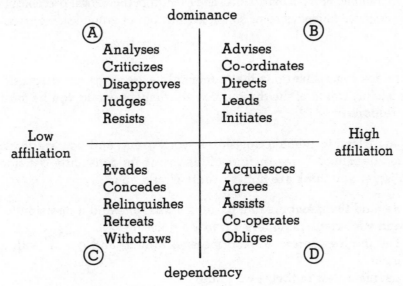

Each quadrant represents a different combination of dominance *v.* dependency — which are self-explanatory facets of behaviour in groups — and high affiliation *v.* low affiliation, which simply means the desire of the person to get along with others. So a group leader or group member who scored high in the top left-hand box — square A — would be a person who dominated or tried to dominate the group and appeared to be unconcerned whether the other members approved or disapproved, liked or disliked what he/she was doing. Someone with a high score in the bottom right-hand corner — square D — would be eager to please at all costs, conforming to the views and manners of the more dominant members.

Very few people fall into a pure category. It is more usual to have a mixture of responses, but a tendency to one corner or another may suggest something about someone's participatory or leadership style. It is also interesting to see where there are differences in judgements between individual's rating of themselves and those made by third parties who observe the proceedings.

The results may suggest to a group leader the desirability of changing in one direction or another; being a bit less dominant, or a bit more affiliative and concerned for the feelings of the group members.

Group leading styles

Leading a group is not just a mechanical process devoid of individual style, it is quite often an extension of the group leader's character or sometimes a consciously adopted and initially alien way of working, derived from the circumstances of the work, from models observed in training, or from experience, and even from theoretical preconceptions. This exercise is designed to look at some simple distinctions of group-leading style.

☐☐ Here are some situations that commonly arise in group discussion. If *you* were the leader, which of the three given alternatives would you be most likely to adopt in response?

1 You are trying to reach a decision in your group and you are working to an agreed deadline. Three or four of the members constantly get side-tracked onto issues you think are not relevant. Would you:

(a) Remind the members that there is a deadline and a decision to be made and encourage members towards a decision?
(b) Tell the 'wanderers' to stop messing around and get on with the job in hand?
(c) Let them stew in their own juice?

2 One of the members of your group talks all the time − it all makes sense but it stops others making their contributions. Do you:

(a) Wait for other group members to put pressure on him/her to reduce the amount of time he/she is talking?
(b) Interrupt the 'talker' and redirect the discussion towards other people?
(c) Tell the 'talker' to give other people a look in?

3 Two members of your group never speak at all, or only in reply to questions directed at them personally by someone else. You think they have a contribution to make to the discussion. Which of the following responses would you be most likely to make?

(a) 'John/Jane, I've noticed that you haven't been making much contribution to the discussion. I think we would get on better if everyone gave their views and helped to produce a decision as quickly as possible.'
(b) 'I think it would be useful if as many people as possible took part in making this decision; does anyone else want to say something about this point?'
(c) Say nothing.

4 Two conflicting points of view have developed in your group and their supporters just repeat them. There is no sign of an agreement emerging. Would you:

(a) Wait and see what happened?
(b) Set out the areas of agreement and disagreement as you saw them in the hope that some common ground would emerge/ask for ideas from the group about how to solve the impasse?
(c) Tell the group that they *have* to reach an agreement of some sort by the deadline now fast approaching?

5 Two of the group members are hostile to one another and although they are not stopping the group working on the decision it has to make, they are making the atmosphere tense and difficult. Do you:

(a) Ask them both to leave so that you can get on with the job in hand?
(b) Hope that other members of the group will ignore them, or if things become too disruptive, say something to the warring parties?
(c) Point out to the two members that their behaviour is having certain effects on the atmosphere of the discussion and invite them to think whether they are being unfair to the other members?

6 One of the group members seems to be personally hostile to everything you say or do as group leader. Would you:

(a) Ignore him/her?

(b) Deal with his/her objections factually and politely and encourage the group to continue with its work?

(c) Tell the member to stop attacking you and let everyone get on with the job?

These questions and their responses are designed to illustrate three contrasting styles of group leadership: (1) directive, (2) laisser-faire, and (3) democratic.

A 'directive' group leader is one who concentrates on the job in hand and makes a lot of interventions to keep the nose of the group to the collective grindstone, stands no nonsense between members or between members and leader, and, as often as not, produces the required results on time, even at the price of a few ruffled feathers in the flock.

A laisser-faire group leader is one with a passionate (if that is not too strong a word) attachment to the idea that groups must manage their own affairs as far as possible. A leader might have to intervene if one member started hitting another, but otherwise groups have to find their own level; all the members and the leader are on an equal footing.

A 'democratic' group leader falls somewhere between the other two styles, trying to encourage everyone in the group to take part and committed to the belief that disagreement can be resolved with patience and tact.

Each of the six questions can be answered in one of these ways; the key below sets out the orientation of the three responses in each case.

Group leading styles: key

Question 1
1 Democratic
2 Directive
3 Laisser-faire

Question 2
1 Laisser-faire
2 Democratic
3 Directive

Question 3
1 Directive
2 Democratic
3 Laisser-faire

Question 4
1 Laisser-faire
2 Democratic
3 Directive

Question 5
1 Directive
2 Laisser-faire
3 Democratic

Question 6
1 Laisser-faire
2 Democratic
3 Directive

This exercise can be conducted in a more open-ended fashion by posing the problems 1–6 and inviting respondents to write out in their own words what they would say in those circumstances. When all the items have been completed the completed answers can then be scored as *directive*, *democratic*, or *laisser-faire*. Taken to extremes the directive and laisser-faire styles of group leadership lead to dependence and rebellion on the one hand and abstention on the other (White and Lippitt 1960). A balanced style – the 'democratic' – falls nicely between these opposites, creating a friendlier and more productive environment than either of them. Such a style is, however, a counsel of perfection and most group leaders are likely to combine elements of all three in their more mundane performances.

□□ Group leader profile

Below is a set of adjectives which describe some qualities thought to be important in the leading of groups. They are arranged as pairs of opposites, with rating scales between them, so that you can rate yourself:

Active	|�⎯⎯⎯| Passive
Non-assertive		Assertive
Talkative		Quiet
Destructive		Constructive
Contributing		Non-contributing
Controlling		Laisser-faire
Negative		Positive
Questioning		Non-questioning
Cold		Warm
Fair		Biased
Task-oriented		Group-oriented
. . . .		. . . .
. . . .		. . . .

Complete the rating scales for yourself as you think you currently operate as a group leader, putting a ring round one point on each dimension. Then, not looking at the first completion, fill it in again, this time for an ideal group leader, and thirdly for the group leader you think you could become.

If you think that the adjectives above do not fully represent the dimensions along which you would like to measure your own group leading performance, add further words of your own choice.

Handling problems in groups

From time to time there are things that go wrong in groups. One set of problems has to do with contribution rates – whether members speak too much or too little. Different kinds of difficulty are encountered along a dimension that runs from 'fight' at one extreme to 'flight' at the other: problems of aggression and withdrawal, in other words. The ability to cope calmly and constructively with sticky situations like these is a key part of the skilled group leader's repertoire.

□□ The exercises that follow are designed to provide practice in dealing with problems of both kinds.

All the exercises except the last one are based on a group of six people, one of them acting as group leader or organizer, and the other five as members. In each case 'briefings' are given to the group members which indicate how they are to behave during the discussion. Some of them are 'normal' members, keen to participate and sensible in what they say; others are 'problem' members briefed to act in different and difficult ways so as to pose a problem for the person leading the group.

The leader leads a group discussion for ten minutes on topic of mutual interest, which the group chooses from a list presented to them, for example:

Summer holidays
Bad habits
Marriage
Newspapers
Religion
The economy

When the leader perceives who is/are the problem person/people in the group, he/she should take appropriate action.

☐ **Silent members**
The following briefings are given to group members:

Member 1. You are a keen and committed member of this group and you contribute information and other helpful comments as appropriate, and you listen to what others have to say and respond to them.
(This is the 'normal' group member briefing which is given to all but the 'problem' individuals.)
Member 2. 'Normal' briefing.
Member 3. You are a very shy person and although you enjoy being in the group and listening to what other people have to say, you never make any contributions yourself, replying only to questions directed at you personally, and then with single-word replies so far as possible. You should avoid being drawn into long statements or revelations of your personal views, which are not in any case very strong ones.

Member 4. You are not a very talkative person and tend to speak only now and then, when you feel that you have something important to contribute.
Member 5. 'Normal' briefing.

☐ Compulsive talkers

In this exercise 'normal' role briefings are distributed to all the group members except *two*, who are each given the following instructions:

> You are a dominant and bossy sort of person who enjoys the sound of your own voice. You have an opinion about everything and are keen to air it and will brook no interruptions or attempts to shut you up. You pause at the end of a contribution but do not listen to or respond to what other people say. You ignore them as far as possible and say what you think is important.

The group leader's job in this situation is to manage a group where there are two compulsive talkers.

☐ Aggression between members

In this exercise, all the members are given 'normal' briefings except two who are given the following:

(a) There is someone else in this group who really dislikes you and picks on you all the time, criticizing what you say, and trying to interrupt when you have something to say. You resent this a lot and fight back with personal criticisms and counter-interruptions.

(b) There is someone in this group you really dislike, and who talks nonsense most of the time. You criticize what he/she says, interrupt when he/she speaks, and try to get the rest of the group to take no notice of him/her. (Whoever is running this exercise should make clear to (b) that (a) is the target of his/her dislike.)

In this situation the group leader has to cope with antagonisms between two members.

☐ Attacking the leader

In this exercise all the members are given 'normal' briefings except one who is given the following:

> You dislike the leader of this group, who is not, in your opinion, leading the group very well. You attack whatever the leader says and try to get other people to join in. You restrict your attacks to the behaviour of the leader in the group.

☐ **Take-over bid**

In this exercise everyone is given a 'normal' briefing except one person who is told:

> You think that the group leader is leading the group astray and that you could do the job better. You take it on yourself to summarize what other people are saying, to encourage the group discussion in directions you think best, to ask questions, and encourage contributions from other members, and to ignore as far as possible the efforts of the so-called leader. You are making what amounts to a take-over bid for leadership of the group.

☐ **Group 'Flight'**

In this exercise, *everyone* in the group is given the briefing:

> You enjoy being in this group but Christmas is approaching and you feel in a festive mood. You do not feel like working or talking about the topic proposed by the leader. You would rather have a laugh and friendly chat with your fellow group members.

☐ **Pandemonium!**

In this exercise, which requires seven group members, *all* the 'problem' briefings from the previous exercises are distributed, one per member, so that you have a silent member, a dominant one, two aggressive ones, one who hates the leader, one who wants to be leader, and one who is in festive mood. The group leader will have real problems with this group!

☐☐ **Feedback**

The exercises can be conducted in a number of ways. After ten minutes of discussion and of attempts to cope with the difficult member(s), all the participants can review what went on, commenting on the leader's performance, and making suggestions about alternative or better ways of handling those particular problems.

Alternatively, the proceedings can be recorded on audio or video tape and the playback evaluated both by the leader and the group members. Or − observers can be appointed to watch and provide feedback when the discussion terminates. (If someone has particular difficulties in dealing with one or other of the problem members, then more practice may be called for.)

Take each situation in turn and brain-storm strategies for dealing with it; things to do and things to say. Ask for examples from the past experience of those taking part in the exercise and how they coped. Rerun the discussions with other 'leaders' modelling different or more adequate approaches to difficult group members.

Some suggestions for dealing with difficulties in groups

There are of course no 'correct' answers in the search for ways of coping with problems in groups, but there are some common-sense things to do in situations of 'fight' and 'flight'.

'FIGHT'

Within certain limits conflict can be a good thing in a group; a vigorous clashing of views and personalities. But there is a point beyond which the vigour turns to aggression and the noise of the clashing drowns out the rest of the conversation.

What to do

1 Don't panic. Quite often such conflicts solve themselves.
2 Let the group solve it. Group pressure on the warring parties may cool things down.
3 Talk to the individuals privately about it. They may welcome a chance to discuss things and to change their future behaviour in the group.
4 In the end you may decide to ask someone to leave for the good of the rest of the group. But discuss it with them all first. They may have some positive suggestions to make.

'FLIGHT'

Flight is an easier thing to manage. A member may ask to leave. Find out if there is any reason for his or her leaving that can be put right. If not, let him or her go. The other kind of flight is where the member stays physically in the group and makes no move to leave but appears to be taking no part in the proceedings and to be getting no benefit from them. Again the group will put pressure on this type of member. If that does not work, a conflict situation may arise which should be dealt with as above. Otherwise, if the silent member is not a disturbing influence on others and appears to be getting something from the discussion, there is no need to take any action.

Problem groups

Occasionally a whole group will fall into fight or flight behaviour, fighting with everyone in sight or fleeing from any kind of constructive activity. When this happens without warning, and for no apparent good reason:

1 Try not to worry too much.
2 There may be virtually nothing you can do.
3 Keep cool and sit it out.

Almost always the group will be in a better mood in the following session, or the session after that. If it goes on longer there may be something seriously wrong. If the problem is one of the group slowly sinking into apathy there may be several solutions:

1 Ask the group what the problem is.
2 Tighten up your programme, or put some spice in it – they may just be bored.
3 Challenge the group to work harder.

Summarizing

Finally, as in interviewing and counselling, it falls to the group leader to summarize the discussion. This serves several purposes: it assures the members of the group that at least one person has been listening to what has been said; it consolidates areas of agreement; indicates topics on which there is disagreement or on which further work is needed; and gives the group a sense of having arrived somewhere, even though it may prove only a temporary resting place on the way to a more distant destination.

Summaries are produced at short notice and 'off the cuff' so they will never be perfect literary productions, for example:

'Well, I think we've gone as far as we can in this discussion of boredom. We've covered a lot of ground – the reasons why people get bored; whether it's because of the lack of things to do where they live, or whether it's really their own fault for sitting on their backsides and doing nothing to help themselves. I don't think we really agreed on that one – some people think bored people have only themselves to blame, and other people think "the system" is at fault for not providing more amenities and leisure facilities for young people in particular. We decided to have a closer look at what there is to do in this neighbourhood and one suggestion was that we make a list of "free" activities and facilities. We also came to the conclusion that we should look more closely at the feelings we have that we call boredom.

'On balance I thought it was a good session; a lot of members said things and there was only one little bit of trouble. Thank you all for coming; see you next Thursday.'

The skill of summarizing a discussion can be developed in several ways.

☐ Tape record a brief discussion that you have led, including your summary. Listen to the discussion only, several days later, and record another summary. Compare the two versions to see if there are any changes in content or style.

☐ Invite an observer to watch you in action leading a group discussion. At the end of the proceedings, you both prepare and write down independent summaries and compare them.

☐ With another person, listen to one round of replies to a question on the radio programme 'Any Questions'; write down independent summaries and compare them.

A self-monitoring schedule for group leaders

Like any other skills, those of leading groups can only be improved by constant practice. This, to be at all effective, must be directed towards particular learning goals, must be done in a self-aware way, and must gather information or feedback about the quality of the work being done.

The most straightforward method for gathering this kind of information is for the learner to reflect on his or her practice in as organized a fashion as possible. Here are some general categories and specific questions for doing this; they are not the only questions that can be asked but they can be used as a basis for reviewing performance.

PREPARATION

On reflection was it a good idea to have organized this particular group? Were the aims that you formulated for the group the right ones? If not, what should they have been? Or could you have made them clearer in some way to the intending participants? Did the aims change as the group continued? Was that a good thing or a bad thing? Were members of the group aware that the agenda was changing?

RECRUITMENT

How effective was the recruitment to the group? Did enough people turn up? Did enough of them stay to make the proceedings viable? How could recruitment be improved in the future? Would other methods have been useful? Did colleagues co-operate in finding people? Could they have done more, and if they didn't, why didn't they?

GROUP COMPOSITION

Was there a balance of characters in the group that helped the proceedings? How would you describe the people who turned up? Did they form natural alliances or groupings? Were there endemic hostilities between members? Could these have been foreseen in advance? Was there anyone who with hindsight it would have been better not to have had as a group member? Can you think of any possible members who would have improved the work or life of the group? Who are they and what would they have brought to the group that was missing? Were some of the members quite different in the group to what you expected, for example more or less quiet, more or less assertive, more or less agreeable?

STARTING OFF

Did the group get off to a good start? Were you reasonably happy with the first session? Were there any hitches or gross problems early on? Did you manage to put people at their ease quickly? Did most people contribute during the first session? Did you explain the purpose clearly, and did the members appear to respond positively to what you were saying? Could you have said something different or said what you did say better, for example in a more lively or stimulating fashion?

WHO SPOKE

Looking back were there any specially dominant members? Any specially silent ones? What was the balance of contribution between yourself and the remainder of the group? Were you happy with it? Did this change during the course of the group? In what ways? Were the silent ones happy at what was happening? Would they have spoken more under other circumstances? Like what? Were many of the contributions directed just between two or three interested parties or was there a wider spread?

WHAT PEOPLE SAID

How would you describe the content of what was said? Does it fall into categories relevant to the major topic? Or not? If not, why not? What was the content of the non-relevant contributions? Were they helpful or otherwise to the group in its deliberations? Were the helpful contributions made by the same person or persons or were they distributed around the membership of the group? Was there any reason for any individual to be persistently unhelpful? Were some of the sessions better than others in terms of what was actually said? Can you identify any reasons for that?

ATMOSPHERE

What was the climate of the group like in each session? Is it possible to describe in a word or phrase the prevailing climate of the group? Or if there were two or three distinct climates, how would you encapsulate each of them in a phrase? How would your group members describe the climate, do you think? The same as you or differently? Why? Were there any sharp swings in the climate of the group and what caused them?

PROBLEMS

Were there any problems in the group? What were they? Did they have to do with you; all the members; specific members; one member? Could they have been avoided altogether? How did you cope with the problems? Could you have done better? If similar problems occur again how do you think you will handle them? Were there any problems that couldn't be solved at all? How aware were the members of the problems you perceived? Did you cause any problems for anyone? What do you need to do to improve your ability to manage problems in groups?

OUTCOMES

Make a list of the outcomes of the group experience, using some of these categories:

— Decisions made. Number, nature, quality, degree of support, feasibility, etc.
— Information exchanged between members of the group.
— Changes in attitude reported or obvious in group members' statements.
— Any discernible changes in behaviour within the group, e.g. amount or quality of verbal contributions, increased self-confidence, greater articulacy, etc.
— Any reported changes in behaviour or situation outside the group.

The precise questions you can ask yourself under any of these headings will depend on the group you planned and ran; you can obviously add others to suit the circumstances. You can simply think about each of these issues and what you would reply to them. You could make some notes or write up a final report on the group following this outline. You could discuss the group with a colleague using this or another framework (Douglas 1976), or you could invite a non-involved colleague to interview you about the group and how it had gone. The colleague could of course expand any of the questions and pursue what appear to be important aspects of the group and your performance.

Group members' evaluation sheet

The most direct form of feedback on a group-leading performance is to be gained from the group members themselves. A general review following a group session can elicit some of their opinions, although politeness and consideration may blunt their critical sharpness. A colleague can interview members separately afterwards but this is time-consuming and not always practicable. A more economical way of collecting this information is through the use of simple evaluation sheets to be filled in (anonymously or otherwise) by group members at the end of the session or series of sessions.

☐☐ The format given here is a very general one to be adapted and added to to fit particular groups, or to look at specific aspects of the group leader's skill.

Group _____   Date _____

1 What do you think the aims of this group were?
2 How far do you think these aims have been achieved?

   Completely ∟_____ı_____ı_____ı_____ı_____ı Not at all

3 Which of the following words would you use to describe the atmosphere in the group sessions?

Warm	Friendly	Active	Productive	Time wasting
Boring	All right	Anxious	Frustrating	Pleasant
Relaxed	Tense	Average	Amusing	Business-like

4 How did you get on with the other group members? Underline the statement you most agree with.

Extremely well   Very well   Quite well   Not too well   Not at all well

5 How well prepared was the group leader for running the group?

10   20   30   40   50   60   70   80   90   100%

Underline the percentage figure you agree with.
6 Describe the way the group has been run in not more than three or four words.
7 How useful has the group been to you?

Not much ⌊_____⌊_____⌊_____⌊_____⌊_____⌋ A lot

8 What do you think you have gained from being a member of this group?
9 Three things you liked; three things you disliked.

Notes and references

Groups are blessed with an enormous literature, not all of it, unfortunately, all that helpful to the beginner in the field. Some good starting places might be with A. Brown (1979) *Groupwork* (London: Heinemann), or T. Douglas (1976) *Groupwork Practice* (London: Tavistock). A very practical introduction to the general skills of working in groups is provided by M. B. Miles (1959) *Learning to Work in Groups* (New York: Teachers College Press). For an example of deliberately elitist writing on groups see W. R. Bion (1970) *Attention and Interpretation* (London: Tavistock).

The best primer of psychological studies of what goes on in groups is still D. Cartwright and A. Zander (1953) (eds) *Group Dynamics: Research and Theory* (London: Tavistock). Categories for recording and classifying contributions to group discussion range from the seminal work of R. F. Bales (1950) *Interaction Process Analysis* (Reading, Mass.; Addison-Wesley), to the more recent N. Rackham and T. Morgan (1977) *Behaviour Analysis in Training* (Maidenhead: McGraw-Hill).

Some group workers use what they call 'trust' exercises to develop the atmosphere in their groups. This can lead to false expectations of friendliness which may be counter-productive. Confidence and relaxation in the presence of others have to be earned by experience over a period of time and cannot be short-circuited by a few simple exercises.

If you want to play some games in a group without great hopes of immediate pay-off, a good source is T. Orlick (1978) *The Co-operative Sports and Games Book: Challenge without Competition* (New York: Pantheon Books).

Two books which outline group skills exercises in more detail are D. W. and F. P. Johnson (1975) *Joining Together: Group Theory and Group Skills* (Englewood Cliffs, N.J.: Prentice-Hall), and D. A. Kolb, I. M. Rubin, and J. McIntyre (1974) *Organizational Psychology: An Experiential Approach* (Second edition) (Englewood Cliffs, N.J.: Prentice-Hall).

Helping to learn: a post-script for learners and teachers

To end the book, some suggestions for using the materials presented in the preceding chapters. It will be obvious by now that they do not constitute a ready-made syllabus for producing helpers, to be opened at page one and pursued relentlessly through to the end. They are intended rather as guide-lines for action to be used in a variety of ways by a variety of people. *Teachers* of helpers may be able to extract items which illustrate or augment some of their existing course content. *Students* may wish to use them to fill gaps in the courses they attend or to give direction to aspects of the work they do on practical placements. Established *workers* in helping agencies, either individually or in teams, could look at the quality of their current practice, and, where they think necessary, take steps to improve it. Interested *individuals* could try some of the exercises to see whether their interest survives the experience and leads them to look for more formal training to become helpers. And last but not least, some of the *people* who take their problems to the helping services could try some of the methods for themselves; the diffusion of helping skills more widely amongst the population might turn out to be not only an effective prophylactic but a vital necessity in a time of shrinking welfare budgets.

The materials can be used on a one-off, self-selection basis, or they can be combined in a more systematic fashion to provide a personal programme of skills development. The starting point of such a programme would be to engage in a process of assessment, or *self-assessment*, using some of the exercises drawn from the chapters on interviewing, counselling, or group leading. The choice of topic and of specific exercises will depend on individual interests and learning needs. One of the reasons why people sometimes shy away from the idea of self-assessment is because of the impossibly high standards against which they think they should measure their performance. But when patients want a wound dressed they do not need a surgeon to do the job adequately, a good nursing assistant will do the job just as well, if not better. It is the same in helping; a confident grasp of basic skills will carry the helper through most ordinary situations. So expectations can be pitched at quite modest levels; those of ordinary everyday competence. Equally important, self-assessment is not only about quality – how good you are at doing something; it is also about style – the manner in which you do it. There is of course no commonly accepted standard for judging personal helping styles, but an awareness of one's own manner of working and the ability to change it to suit changing circumstances can be a great asset.

It should also be remembered that the self-consciousness generated by any form of self-assessment is meant to be temporary and to serve the purpose of bringing to light aspects of helping behaviour that may require improving. These should be formulated as specific *learning goals*; for example, to speak less in assessment interviews, to ask more systematic questions, to be more perceptive of how other people are feeling, to express support more directly, to prepare more thoroughly for a group discussion, and to summarize proceedings more succinctly. The goals should be as concrete as you can make them; they should be achievable, and capable of being evaluated; that is, how will you know that they *have* been achieved?

The third and most arduous part of this learning process is achieving goals by any means possible, which will include becoming better informed through lectures and reading, observing skilled performers, thinking about what you are trying to do, discussing it with others, and most critical of all, by *practice*. Practice poses no problems for those already employed as helpers; other learners may face difficulties in securing suitable cases for their first efforts. Fellow students or learners are the most obvious source of subjects for interviewing, counselling, or group leading practice, but they are not a complete answer. Simulated helping situations with friends or colleagues can carry the learner only so far; usually through the basic mechanics of the activity in question. Beyond that they may be so far removed from the reality they attempt to depict, and so fraught with possibilities for falling about laughing, as to offer few learning gains. A little more reality, and a little less levity, can be introduced into the proceedings by recruiting less well-known individuals to be interviewed, or counselled, or whatever. They may be students from another year or another course altogether. They may be workers in helping agencies who are willing to help in this way. They may be sympathetic family members or personal friends, or friends of friends and *their* friends. But, except in rare instances, all these willing helpers are likely to be different in crucial respects from the men and women and children who end up on the case-loads of helping agencies. Efforts must be made therefore to locate people who more nearly resemble those with whom you ultimately intend to work. You may be able to locate them in schools, colleges, clubs, or youth employment projects; they may be resident in homes or hostels or penal institutions; some of them are to be found amongst the well-known members of agency case-loads. If the purpose of the exercise is clearly explained to everyone concerned, staff *and* clientele, and the subjects to be tackled are restricted to ones which are not central to the work currently being done with them, there is no reason why practice sessions in such places should not be diverting and educational in both directions.

With only a little imagination and some effort, practice opportunities can be organized into a graded series that leads from role-play between fellow learners to encounters that are indistinguishable from the real thing. This permits skill and confidence to be consolidated at each level of reality and difficulty, before the next step in the progression is attempted.

At some point, practice passes into real work, but that need not be a signal for the learning process to terminate; there is always something in a helping performance that can be bettered and a truly skilful helper is constantly refining and improving what he or she does with people.

The key to this continuous polishing is the use of *self-monitoring* and *evaluation* methods to furnish the learner with *feedback* from as many sources as practicable. This can be done by viewing video tapes of yourself in action; by asking for the views of independent observers; and, most threatening of all, by soliciting the opinions of the people on the receiving end of your helping efforts. It may all appear to constitute an exacting self-discipline but it is the only way of offering a progressively better service to those who patronize your place of work. And it simply makes explicit a process which happens anyway, usually at a tacit and therefore less useful level of awareness.

Finally, the materials themselves should not be seen as finished products immutably linked to the topics and situations set out in the various chapters of the book, which have been selected simply as *illustrations*. They can be adapted and changed in any of a number of ways. First, the nature of the illustrations can be altered to refer to medical issues, drugs, rights, education, vocational preparation, or whatever is relevant to particular learners. Second, the methods used in one section can equally be applied to other areas of skills like interviewing, counselling, or group leading. And third, materials like these could be developed and applied to additional helping skills; rights advocacy, for example, residential work, running activity groups, helping self-help groups, community work, or social skills training. In all of these areas it is possible to identify skills and their sub-skills and to invent exercises which promote improvements in individual performances of them. This is of course a time-consuming business demanding imagination as well as application, but the task of writing training materials can be an education in itself for both solo workers *and* the teams to which they belong.

So in the end we see this book and its contents as a starting point rather than a finishing line; a stimulus to self-help and self-development rather than a definitive curriculum. We hope you will find it useful.

References

Argyle, M. (1975) *Bodily Communication*. London: Methuen.
—— (1978) *The Psychology of Interpersonal Behaviour*. (Third edition). Harmondsworth: Penguin.
Argyle, M., Alkema, F. and Gilmour, R. (1972) The communication of friendly and hostile attitudes by verbal and non-verbal signals. *European Journal of Social Psychology* **1**: 385–402.
Argyle, M. and Cook, M. (1976) *Gaze and Mutual Gaze*. London: Cambridge University Press.
Bales, R. F. (1950) *Interaction Process Analysis*. Reading, Mass.: Addison-Wesley.
Bandura, A. (1962) Social learning through imitation. In M. R. Jones (ed.) *Nebraska Symposium on Motivation*. Lincoln, Neb.: University of Nebraska Press. Pp. 211–69.
Bion, W. R. (1970) *Attention and Interpretation*. London: Tavistock.
Bolger, A. W. (1982) (ed.) *Counselling in Britain: a reader*. London: Batsford.
Brown, A. (1979) *Groupwork*. London: Heinemann.
Brown, G. (1975) *Microteaching: a programme of teaching skills*. London: Methuen.
—— (1979) *Lecturing and Explaining*. London: Methuen.
Carkhuff, R. R. (1969) *Helping and Human Relations*. Vols 1 and 2. New York: Holt, Rinehart, and Winston.
Cartwright, D. and Zander, A. (1953) (eds) *Group Dynamics: Research and Theory*. London: Tavistock.
CODOT *Classification of Occupations and Directory of Occupational Titles* (Vols 1, 2, and 3). London: HMSO.
Culbertson, F. M. (1957) Modification of an emotionally held attitude through role-playing. *Journal of Abnormal and Social Psychology* **54**: 230–33.

Dominian, J. (1968) *Marital Breakdown*. Harmondsworth: Penguin.

Douglas, T. (1976) *Groupwork Practice*. London: Tavistock.

Egan, G. (1981) *The Skilled Helper*. Monterey, Cal.: Brooks-Cole.

Ellis, R. (1980) Simulated social skill training for interpersonal professions. In W. T. Singleton, P. Spurgeon, and R. B. Stammers (eds) *The Analysis of Social Skill*. New York: Plenum Press. Pp. 79–101.

Eysenck, H. J. (1953) *Uses and Abuses of Psychology*. Harmondsworth: Penguin.

Falloon, I., Lindley, P., and McDonald, R. (1974) *Social Training: a manual*. London: Psychological Treatment Section, Maudsley Hospital.

Frank, S. J. (1978) Just imagine how I feel: how to improve empathy through training in imagination. In J. L. Singer and K. S. Pope (eds) *The Power of Human Imagination: new methods in psychotherapy*. New York: Plenum Press. Pp. 309–46.

Fraser, J. M. (1971) *Introduction to Personnel Management*. London: Nelson.

Garfinkel, H. (1967) *Studies in Ethnomethodology*. Englewood Cliffs, N.J.: Prentice-Hall.

Goldstein, A. P., Sprafkin, R. P., and Gershaw, N. J. (1976) *Skill Training for Community Living*. New York: Pergamon Press/Structured Learning Associates.

Gough, H. G. (1957) *Manual for the California Psychological Inventory*. Palo Alto, Cal.: Consulting Psychologists' Press.

Hall, A. S. (1975) *The Point of Entry*. London: Allen and Unwin.

Hamblin, D. (1974) *The Teacher and Counselling*. Oxford: Blackwell.

Hargie, O., Saunders, C., and Dickson, D. (1981) *Social Skills in Interpersonal Communication*. London: Croom Helm.

Heller, K. (1972) Interview structure and interviewer style in initial interviews. In A. W. Siegman and B. Pope (eds) *Studies in Dyadic Communication*. New York: Pergamon.

Hopson, B. and Hayes, J. (1968) (eds) *The Theory and Practice of Vocational Guidance*. Oxford: Pergamon.

Hugman, B. (1977) *Act Natural*. London: Bedford Square Press.

Ivey, A. E. and Authier, J. (1978) *Microcounselling*. Springfield, Ill.: Charles C. Thomas.

Ivey, A. E. and Simek-Downing, L. (1980) *Counselling and Psychotherapy: Skills, Theories, and Practice*. Englewood Cliffs, N.J.: Prentice-Hall.

Johnson, D. W. and Johnson, F. P. (1975) *Joining Together: Group Theory and Group Skills*. Englewood Cliffs, N.J.: Prentice-Hall.

Jordan, B. (1979) *Helping in Social Work*. London: Routledge and Kegan Paul.

Jourard, S. (1964) *The Transparent Self*. New York: Van Nostrand.

—— (1971) *Self-disclosure*. New York: Wiley.

Jourard, S. and Jaffe, P. E. (1970) Influence of an interviewer's disclosure on the self-disclosure of interviewees. *Journal of Counselling Psychology* 17: 252–59.

Kanfer, F. H. and Goldstein, A. P. (1980) (eds) *Helping People Change: a text-book of methods*. Oxford: Pergamon.

Knapp, M. L. (1980) *Essentials of Non-verbal Communication*. New York: Holt, Rinehart, and Winston.

Kolb, D. A. and Boyatzis, R. E. (1974). On the dynamics of the helping relationship. In D. A. Kolb, I. M. Rubin, and J. M. McIntyre (eds) *Organisational Psychology: a book of readings*. Englewood Cliffs, N.J.: Prentice-Hall. Pp. 371–87.

Kolb, D. A., Rubin, I. M., and McIntyre, J. M. (1974) *Organisational Psychology: An Experiential Approach*. (Second edition). Englewood Cliffs, N.J.: Prentice-Hall.

Krumboltz, J. D. and Thoresen, C. E. (1976) (eds) *Counselling Methods*. New York: Holt, Rinehart, and Winston.

Kübler-Ross, E. (1969) *On Death and Dying*. London: Tavistock.

Lefcourt, H. M. (1976) *Locus of Control: current trends in theory and research*. Hillsdale, N.J.: Lawrence Erlbaum Associates.

MacShane, D. (1979) *Using the Media*. London: Pluto Press.

Mager, R. F. and Pipe, P. (1970), *Analysing Performance Problems*. Belmont, Cal.: Fearon Publishers.

Matarazzo, R. G. (1978) Research on the teaching and learning of psychotherapeutic skills. In S. L. Garfield and A. E. Bergin (eds) *Handbook of Psychotherapy and Behaviour Change*. New York: Wiley. Pp. 941–66.

McGuire, D., Thelen, M. H., and Amolsch, T. (1975) Interview self-disclosure as a function of length of modelling and descriptive instructions. *Journal of Consulting and Clinical Psychology* **43**: 356–62.

Miles, M. B. (1959) *Learning to work in groups*. New York: Teachers College Press.

Morris, D. (1977) *Manwatching*. London: Jonathan Cape.

Munro, E. A., Manthei, R. J., and Small, J. J. (1979) *Counselling: a Skills Approach*. Wellington: Methuen (New Zealand).

Nelson-Jones, R. (1982) *The Theory and Practice of Counselling Psychology*. Eastbourne: Holt, Rinehart, and Winston.

Orlick, T. (1978) *The Cooperative Sports and Games Book: Challenge without Competition*. New York: Pantheon Books.

Orlinsky, D. E. and Howard, K. I. (1978) The relation of process to outcome in psychotherapy. In S. L. Garfield and A. E. Bergin (eds) *Handbook of Psychotherapy and Behaviour Change*. New York: Wiley. Pp. 283–329.

Parloff, M. B., Waskow, I. E., and Wolfe, B. E. (1978) Research on therapist variables in relation to process and outcome. In S. L. Garfield and A. E. Bergin (eds) *Handbook of Psychotherapy and Behaviour Change*. New York: Wiley. Pp. 233–82.

Parsloe, P. (1981) *Social Services Area Teams*. London: Allen and Unwin.

Rackham, N. and Morgan, T. (1977) *Behaviour Analysis in Training*. Maidenhead: McGraw-Hill.

Rice, A. K. (1965) *Learning for Leadership: Interpersonal and Intergroup Relations*. London: Tavistock.

Rodger, A. (1974) *Seven Point Plan*. London: National Foundation for Educational Research.

Rogers, C. R. (1951) *Client-Centered Therapy*. Boston, Mass.: Houghton Mifflin.

—— (1957) The necessary and sufficient conditions of therapeutic personality change. *Journal of Consulting Psychology* **21**: 95–103.

—— (1961) *On Becoming a Person*. Boston, Mass.: Houghton Mifflin.

Rogers, J. M. (1960) Operant conditioning in a quasi-therapy setting. *Journal of Abnormal and Social Psychology* **60**: 247–52.

Rotter, J. B. (1954) *Social Learning and Clinical Psychology*. Englewood Cliffs, N.J.: Prentice-Hall.

—— (1966) Generalized expectancies for internal versus external control of reinforcement. *Psychological Monographs* **80** (Whole No. 609).

Schweinitz, E. de and Schweinitz, K. de (1962) *Interviewing in the Social Services: an introduction*. London: National Council of Social Service.

Seymour, W. D. (1966) *Industrial Skills*. London: Pitman.

Sidney, E., Brown, M., and Argyle, M. (1973) *Skills With People*. London: Hutchinson.

Simon, S., Howe, L., and Kirschenbaum, H. (1972) *Values Clarification*. New York: Hart.

Stone, G. L. and Gotlib, I. (1975) Effect of instructions and modelling on self-disclosure. *Journal of Counselling Psychology* **22**: 288–93.

Toukmanian, S. G. and Rennie, D. L. (1975) Microcounselling versus human relations training: relative effectiveness with undergraduate trainees. *Journal of Counselling Psychology* **22**: 345–52.

Towle, C. (1954) *The Learner in Education for the Professions*. Chicago: Chicago University Press.

Trower, P., Bryant, B., and Argyle, M. (1978). *Social Skills and Mental Health*. London: Methuen.

Truax, C. B. and Carkhuff, R. R. (1967) *Toward Effective Counselling and Psychotherapy*. Chicago: Aldine.

Turrell, M. (1980) *Training Analysis*. Plymouth: MacDonald and Evans.

Uhlemann, M. R., Lea, G. W., and Stone, G. L. (1976) Effect of instructions and modelling on trainees low in interpersonal-communication skills. *Journal of Counselling Psychology* **23**: 509–13.

Vernon, T. (1980) *Gobbledegook: a critical review of official forms and leaflets – and how to improve them*. London: National Consumer Council.

Verplanck, W. S. (1955) The control of the content of conversation: reinforcement of statements of opinion. *Journal of Abnormal and Social Psychology* **51**: 668–76.

White, R. and Lippitt, R. (1968) Leader behaviour and member reaction in three 'social climates'. In D. Cartwright and A. Zander (eds) *Group Dynamics: Research and Theory*. London: Tavistock. Pp. 318–35.

Wiener, N. (1950) *The Human Use of Human Beings*. New York: Doubleday.

Wright, D. S. (1971) *The Psychology of Moral Behaviour*. Harmondsworth: Penguin.

Yelloly, M. (1972) The helping relationship. In D. Jehu, P. Hardiker, M. Yelloly, and M. Shaw (eds) *Behaviour Modification in Social Work*. Chichester: Wiley.

—— (1980) *Social Work Theory and Psychoanalysis*. New York: Van Nostrand.

Index